Other Books by

CHRISTOPHER LASCH

―――――――――――

The American Liberals and the Russian Revolution
[1962]

The New Radicalism in America
[1965]

THE
AGONY OF THE
AMERICAN LEFT

The
AGONY OF THE
AMERICAN LEFT

CHRISTOPHER LASCH

New York / Alfred · A · Knopf / 1969

80610

Library of Congress Catalog Card Number: 69-10708

THIS IS A BORZOI BOOK
PUBLISHED BY ALFRED A. KNOPF, INC.

"The Decline of Populism" originally appeared in slightly different form in *Katallagete*, Journal of the Committee of Southern Churchmen.

"The Collapse of Socialism and the Isolation of the Intellectuals," "Black Power: Cultural Nationalism as Politics," and "The Revival of Political Controversy in the Sixties" originally appeared in slightly different form in *The New York Review of Books*.

"The Cultural Cold War: A Short History of the Congress for Cultural Freedom" originally appeared in slightly different form in *The Nation*.

FIRST EDITION

TO

ROBBY

PREFACE

We now have the abnormal situation that, in the face of the
extraordinary novelties and complexities of modern times,
there is no persuasive program for social reconstruction,
thought up by many minds, corrected by endless criticism,
made practical by much political activity. . . . The young are
honorable and see the problems, but they don't know anything because we have not taught them anything.
 —Paul Goodman, *The New York Times Magazine,*
 February 25, 1968

WHAT EXPLAINS THIS "ABNORMAL SITUATION"? WHY
 do we find ourselves, in an unprecedented crisis
 in our history, without a program for change?
Goodman attributes this condition to "the failure of the
intellectuals during the late forties and fifties," who "allowed
themselves to be 'co-opted' by the C.I.A., the Rand Corporation, [and] the universities," in which they "were kept busy,
were able to esteem themselves as in the swim and thereby
did not devote themselves to their normal business—to create
new programs for the future."
It is true that the defection of intellectuals in the period

just past is the immediate source of our troubles. In one of the following essays, "The Cultural Cold War," I have analyzed this defection from the point of view of one who came intellectually of age in the fifties, when the official "realism" was the dominant ideology. My experience and the experience of many of my friends and contemporaries fully bears out the contention that the intellectuals' acquiescence in the premises of the cold war made it unusually difficult to get a political education in the fifties.

The deeper explanation of the present crisis of radicalism, however, lies in events that happened in the early part of this century. It lies in the collapse of mass-based radical movements which grew for a time and then aborted: populism, socialism, and black nationalism. The essays in this book deal with the promising beginnings made by those movements, with the reasons for their failure, and with the consequences of that failure.

Those who wish to change America must now pick up the thread of radical thought and action where it was broken, not in the thirties and forties, but in an even more distant period. The men of that time speak to us across intervening generations of silence, and it is often hard to understand what they are saying. Moreover modern history unfolds so rapidly that the distance between generations is more than normally wide. Many young people today see no use in the past, perhaps because the immediate past has had so little to teach them. The history of American radicalism, in any case, is largely a history of failure and therefore not a source of comfort to those who look to the past to find ancestors and heroes. All that we find in the past of American radicalism are ordinary men and women struggling with questions which the best of them realized were too difficult to resolve but which nevertheless seemed to demand a continuing effort to resolve them. Radicalism in the United States has no great triumphs to record; but the sooner we begin to understand why this should be so, the sooner we will be able to change it.

Three editors, James Y. Holloway of *Katallagete,* Carey McWilliams of *The Nation,* and Robert Silvers of the *New York Review of Books,* gave me invaluable advice and assistance in the writing of one or the other of these essays. I thank them all. Bob Silvers in particular has been a generous and exacting critic, and although I have not found it easy even to approximate his standards, I am grateful to him for insisting on them.

I should also like to acknowledge once again my obligation to Harold Cruse's *The Crisis of the Negro Intellectual,* which has been an indispensable guide through the complexities of American cultural history. Although this work continues to be deliberately ignored by reviewers, it will eventually come to be regarded as one of the landmarks of social criticism in the twentieth century.

CONTENTS

These young intellectuals are the victims of historical discontinuity. . . . As a result, this new generation is called upon to make up for lost time—about forty-five years of it.
—Harold Cruse, *The Crisis of the Negro Intellectual*

THE DECLINE
OF POPULISM

THE EIGHTY YEARS BETWEEN THE CIVIL WAR AND THE Second World War appear in retrospect as a distinctive epoch of American life. During those years the antebellum agrarian order gave way to an industrial economy which by the time of the First World War had already become the most advanced in the world. The geographical concentration of industry at strategic points in the railway network gave rise to enormous cities, at once squalid and vibrant, the bane of democracy and the "hope of democracy."[1] Giant corporations displaced individual entrepreneurs in industry after industry, gradually extending their sway over almost the whole of American life—but not before a succession of immigrant groups had exploited the remaining opportunities in marginal areas of American capitalism, not yet dominated by corporations, to advance from poverty to relative well-being.[2] The drying-up of entrepreneurial capitalism and the emergence of a corporate elite perpetuating itself through the accumulation of educational advantages meant that in postindustrial society the remaining poor —black people, Puerto Ricans, Mexican-Americans, migrants from Appalachia—would find themselves locked into pov-

---

[1] See Frederic C. Howe: *The City: The Hope of Democracy* (New York: Charles Scribner's Sons; 1906), Richard T. Ely: *The Coming City* (New York: Thomas Y. Crowell; 1902).

[2] For a discussion of ethnic groups in American society, see below, pp. 134 ff.

[3]

erty, left behind in decaying cities from which earlier prole-
tarians, together with the industries that employed them,
had fled.

During the urban-industrial period of capitalist development, by contrast, poverty was a pervasive rather than a
marginal experience: it immediately affected the lives of
masses of people and played a central part in the consciousness of the period. Repeated and regular cycles of boom
and depression throughout the industrial age left millions
destitute. The depressions of the 1870's and 1890's, no less
than the Great Depression of the 1930's, were major cata-
clysms, while the economic recession of 1911 might well
have deepened into another full-scale depression if war
preparations in 1914 had not acted as an artificial stimu-
lant.[3] These upheavals fell with terrible weight on those
directly involved in the industrial enterprise—on the industrial workers—whereas in our own time poverty has been
eliminated from the sphere of American society dominated
by large corporations and falls on precisely those whom the
system has not assimilated: migrant and seasonal workers,
the chronically unemployed, and workers in the shops of
petty capitalism.

In postindustrial society resistance to the existing order
comes from these groups and from university students, who
for very different reasons have a marginal relationship to

[3] Indeed the entire period from 1907 to 1915 was one of economic
stagnation. "If the First World War had not come along, the decade
1910–1920 would have gone down in United States history as an
extraordinarily depressed one." (Paul A. Baran and Paul M. Sweezy:
Monopoly Capital [New York: Monthly Review Press; 1966], p.
234.) It is not too much to say, therefore, that during the eighty-year
period between 1865 and 1945 (arbitrary dates which roughly indi-
cate the outer limits of the industrial, as distinguished from the pre-
and postindustrial period of American society) there was a built-in
tendency for major depressions to occur at twenty-year intervals.

the dominant institutions of American society. In the industrial period it was people most immediately victimized by those institutions who resisted them—workers, farmers, and their allies in the middle class and among intellectuals. Their efforts to defend themselves against the emerging corporate order gave rise to two distinct political movements, populism and socialism, around which other dissident movements tended to congregate. The People's party and the Socialist party, flourishing respectively in the 1890's and in the period from 1910 to 1919, were particular expressions of a more general discontent which found other outlets as well. Socialist sentiment in the United States was by no means confined to the Socialist party or to its rival, the Socialist Labor party. It found its way into progressivism, into the movement for "social justice," and indeed into populism itself. Similarly the People's party did not represent the limits of populism. The LaFollette wing of the progressive movement represented a variety of populism, as did the Nonpartisan League of North Dakota and the Farmer-Labor party of Minnesota at a somewhat later time. In the industrial period of American history, populism and socialism reflected two broad patterns of opposition to corporate capitalism, occasionally converging but ideologically distinct.[4]

Socialism was consciously revolutionary and conceived

[4] Populist and Marxist rhetoric sometimes coincided. The Populist platform of 1892 contained the ringing declaration: "The fruits of the toil of millions are boldly stolen to build up colossal fortunes for a few, unprecedented in the history of mankind; and the possessors of these, in turn, despise the republic and endanger liberty. From the same prolific womb of governmental injustice we breed the two great classes—tramps and millionaires." Some historians have concluded from this rhetorical coincidence that the Populist critique of capitalism, though arrived at independently, was essentially the same as the Socialist critique. (Norman Pollack: *The Populist Response to Industrial America* [Cambridge: Harvard University Press; 1962.])

of the solution to the "social question" as the overthrow (not necessarily violent) of the bourgeoisie by the working class. The populists were by no means a reactionary movement of the *petit-bourgeoisie*, as the Socialist Laborite Daniel DeLeon maintained, but their ideas derived not from Marx but from the physiocratic tradition and from the democracy of Jefferson, Jackson, and Lincoln. The populists, like the socialists, believed that the "producing classes" should enjoy the fruits of their toil, that the "interests" had appropriated the wealth that rightly belonged to the people, and that the masses should organize in their own defense; but the vagueness of this terminology, compared with the relative precision of the socialist vocabulary, betrayed basic differences of outlook. It was not simply that populists, in theory at least, tended to identify "production" with agriculture and to see land as the ultimate source of wealth. Socialists maintained that not only industrialization but the concentration of industrial production were historically progressive developments leading to the collectivization of production. Populists, on the other hand, regarded them with loathing, as leading to bureaucracy, the fragmentation of experience, and the tyranny of organizations.

The history of the twentieth century suggests that these

This conclusion, as I have argued in the *Pacific Historical Review* (February 1964, pp. 69–73), rests almost entirely on verbal correspondences; it is arrived at by piecing together a series of quotations abstracted from their context and treated with equal weight, without regard for speaker or occasion, so as to form a wholly synthetic system which is then attributed to the Populists themselves. In his *Intellectual Origins of American Radicalism* (New York: Pantheon Books; 1968), Staughton Lynd, using a similar technique that is open to the same objections, tries to show that the populist tradition of Thoreau and other American radicals complemented and was consistent with Marxism.

apprehensions about centralized power had a firm basis in reality. What distinguished populism from socialism was not that the former was reactionary or that the populists were incurable individualists who did not see the need for counter-organization against the power of organized wealth. They favored labor unions and farmers' cooperatives and advocated nationalization of railroad, telephone, and telegraph services. The difference lay rather in their confidence that these changes could be brought about without a fundamental restructuring of American society or a long period of tutelage during which the victims of capitalism would have to be gradually made aware of their victimization not by unscrupulous "interests" but by capitalism itself. The populists lacked the socialist conception of ideology. The Marxian tradition of social thought has always attached great importance to the way in which class interests take on the quality of objective reality, so that the class basis of ideas is concealed both from those whose class interests they support and from those whom they aid in exploiting. Lacking an awareness of the human capacity for collective self-deception, the populists tended to postulate conspiratorial explanations of history. These were by no means the crude fantasies that some historians have seen as the populists' only contribution to political discourse. They could take the form of a sophisticated economic determinism—as in Charles A. Beard's economic interpretation of the Constitution—according to which men consciously manipulate events to serve their immediate personal interests. Many American Marxists have themselves embraced an economic determinism that owes more to the populist tradition than to Marxism, so that it is not surprising if Marxism is so often confused, by Marxists and non-Marxists alike, with the economic interpretation of history. The concept of ideology, however, differs from purely economic interpretations in emphasizing class as opposed to personal interests and in analyzing ideas not as "rationalizations" in the narrow sense of conscious lies but as elaborate structures of thought, permeating the consciousness of entire epochs, which are so closely related to the dominant structures of production that the relationship is no longer a matter for conscious reflection.[5]

The economic interpretation of history, on the other hand, usually assumes that conflicts of interests are open and clear-cut and that an appeal to economic self-interest, therefore, will serve to rally the forces of enlightenment around programs of progressive change. The populists did not appreciate the degree to which dissidence based merely on economic interests (as opposed to the entire social, cultural, economic, and psychological *situation* in which exploited classes find themselves) could be accommodated and absorbed by the corporate system, while leaving the system essentially intact. Nor did they foresee how easily

---

[5] Marxism thus implies a radical break with the psychology of interests, according to which men rationally perceive and act upon their self-interest. (See Karl Mannheim: *Ideology and Utopia* [New York: Harvest Books; n.d.], pp. 57–8.) In this respect the Marxian concept of ideology anticipates and is fully compatible with the determinism of Freud, which, like Marxism, originates in a negation or "contradiction" of common-sense appearances. "Consciousness appears to us as positively the characteristic that defines mental life, and we regard psychology as the study of the content of consciousness. This even appears so evident that any contradiction of it seems obvious nonsense to us, and yet it is impossible for psychoanalysis to avoid this contradiction, or to accept the identity between the conscious and the psychic." According to Freud, the "illusion of psychic freedom" (a "quite unscientific" belief) "must give ground before the claims of a determinism which governs even mental life." (Sigmund Freud: *A General Introduction to Psychoanalysis* [New York: Washington Square Press; 1960], pp. 26, 52, 112.) Similarly Marxism, through a study of ideology, attacks the illusion of psychic freedom and choice.

aroused indignation can lapse back into indifference, once immediate grievances are satisfied. Much more than the socialists, who were geared to a patient long-term effort to create a mass consciousness of the moral superiority of a socialist order, American populists have always been easy prey to disillusionment, when hopes of speedy change turn to dust. This explains why so many populists of the nineties turned into cranky demagogues in their later years—a recurrent pattern in the history of populism.

With all its limitations, populism nevertheless contained great promise, in the years around the turn of the century, of growing into a formidable challenge to corporate capitalism. This fact was recognized by many socialists in the nineties—Laurence Gronlund, Henry Demarest Lloyd, and J. A. Wayland among others—who called for support of the People's party. Even some of DeLeon's followers broke away from the sectarian Socialist Labor party to support populism, on the grounds that "if the co-operative Commonwealth is to be achieved," as one of them put it, "the true reformer must take advantage of every opportunity presented. As the S.L.P. of America can never grow beyond the limit of certain nationalities the cause of socialism will never progress in its present condition."[6] Together the People's party and the Socialist party, the broad and nonsectarian organization that emerged out of the partial collapse of the SLP, represented the beginnings of a mass movement against the dehumanizing effects of the new industrial order.

The dominant liberalism, on the other hand, which most historians have mistakenly seen as the principal twentieth-

---

[6] Joseph B. Keim to New Jersey state central committee, Socialist Labor party, August 25, 1896; quoted in Pollack: *The Populist Response to Industrial America*, p. 101.

century manifestation of popular democracy, actually served the needs of the industrial system. Progressivism, except when it was informed by socialist or populist perspectives, was progressive chiefly in attacking the archaic entrepreneurial capitalism the existence of which impeded the rationalization of American industry. As I have pointed out elsewhere, the new liberalism advocated by Edward A. Ross, Herbert Croly, Richard T. Ely, Newton D. Baker, and even by Jane Addams and John Dewey sought not so much to democratize the industrial system as to make it run more efficiently. These reformers wished to substitute "education" for older and cruder methods of social control, techniques that appeared to them not only offensive in themselves, since they rested on coercion, but inexcusably inefficient. "We are likely to take the influence of superior force for control," John Dewey argued in a characteristic passage, "forgetting that while we may lead a horse to water we cannot make him drink; and that while we can shut a man up in a penitentiary we cannot make him penitent." Even when they originated in humanitarian impulses, progressive ideas led not to a philosophy of liberation but to a blueprint for control. The task of the social reformer came to be seen as that "of enlisting the person's own participating disposition in getting the result desired, and thereby of developing within him an intrinsic and persisting direction in the right way."[7] Manipulative and managerial, twentieth-century liberalism has adapted itself without difficulty to the corporation's need to soften conflicts and to reconcile the apparently irreconcilable forces—capital and labor, bu-

[7] John Dewey: *Democracy and Education* (New York: Macmillan; 1961), pp. 26–7. For a discussion of liberalism as a politics of social control, see Christopher Lasch: *The New Radicalism in America, 1889–1963* (New York: Alfred A. Knopf; 1965), Ch. v.

reaucratic efficiency and personal intimacy, the life of the production line and the life of the spirit—to which it has given rise.

Historians are becoming increasingly conscious of the connection between progressivism and the ascendancy of corporate enterprise. In *The Triumph of Conservatism,* Gabriel Kolko shows that business itself inspired many of the reforms of the progressive era; and the same thing could be said of the reforms of the New Deal. What the corporations needed, and what progressive reformers provided, was "political capitalism": the regulation of competition and the imposition of uniform standards.[8] Similarly, James Weinstein argues in a recent study of progressivism that "the ideal of a liberal corporate social order was formulated and developed under the aegis and supervision of those who then, as now, enjoyed ideological and political hegemony in the United States: the more sophisticated leaders of America's largest corporations and financial institutions."[9] The populist and socialist movements, on the other hand, expressed the needs of people whose lives were controlled by institutions over which they had a steadily diminishing amount of power.

The eventual failure of these movements, therefore, is a matter of highest importance. For in both cases, the promise of the prewar years did not fulfill itself. By the mid-twenties, both socialism and populism had petered out,

[8] Gabriel Kolko: *The Triumph of Conservatism* (New York: Free Press of Glencoe; 1963).

[9] James Weinstein: *The Corporate Ideal in the Liberal State, 1900–1918* (Boston: Beacon Press; 1968), p. ix. See also Loren Baritz: *The Servants of Power* (Middletown, Conn.: Wesleyan University Press; 1960); Robert H. Wiebe: *Businessmen and Reform* (Cambridge: Harvard University Press; 1962).

leaving a political vacuum that has not yet been filled—certainly not by the "new radicalism" of the sixties. Why did these movements collapse? The case of socialism will be examined later.[1] The present essay will concern itself with the decline of populism and of the reform impulse in general. The history of agrarian radicalism, of the labor movement, of the early civil rights movement, and of other campaigns for popular democracy all share certain features in common, which taken together tell us something not only about the recent past but about the prospects for a revival of populism in the future.

[II]

The history of the People's party, which came to fruition in the 1890's and collapsed almost immediately thereafter, offers the clearest example of a pattern which is by no means peculiar to populism. It is a mistake to think of populism as an exclusively agrarian phenomenon. One of the cleavages within the movement, in fact, divided those who wished the People's party to become a vehicle for the special interests of farmers from those who advocated a broad program of reform. The latter group often held temperance, feminism, socialism, and other causes to be as important as agrarian reform. Men like Ignatius Donnelly and Henry Demarest Lloyd advocated a coalition of reform interests, arguing that the plight of the farmer was also the plight of the urban worker, the plight of all those whose interests industrial capitalism had ruthlessly overridden. Similarly Tom Watson of Georgia proposed a combination of Negro

---

[1] See below, pp. 34 ff.

farmers and white, in common revolt against Bourbon domination of the South. In Kansas, as a recent study by Walter Nugent makes clear, a large number of Populists were feminists and prohibitionists as well.[2]

Benjamin Orange Flower, editor of *Arena* and one of the chief spokesmen for populism, exemplifies the kind of reformer who was attracted to populism. The son of a minister, Flower preached from his secular forum, in effect, what later came to be called the social gospel. He supported every progressive cause of the day: the initiative, referendum, and recall; public ownership of utilities; free silver; the interests of labor; prison reform; woman suffrage. His book *Civilization's Inferno, or Studies in the Social Cellar* (1893) was one of the first attempts by an American to subject poverty to systematic description. At the same time and with equal enthusiasm, Flower threw himself into other causes which modern liberals find it hard to accept as liberal or progressive at all, but which one finds running through many reform movements of the late nineteenth century. Not only did he advocate prohibition, a reform from which urban liberals have since dissociated themselves, he was a militant and in later life an obsessive anti-Catholic, endlessly fulminating against "the monarchial and democracy-destroying, upas-like Roman hierarchy, which is in effect a government within our Government, whose theory of rule is in direct opposition to vital and fundamental principles of our liberal democracy."[3]

Finally, Flower dabbled in faith-healing and spiritualism and opposed the efforts of the medical profession to elimi-

[2] Walter T. K. Nugent: *The Tolerant Populists* (Chicago: University of Chicago Press; 1963).

[3] Benjamin Orange Flower: *Righting the People's Wrongs* (Cincinnati: Standard Publishing Company; 1917), p. 5.

nate these marginal elements. It helps to remember that even William James (in whose career many lines of nineteenth-century democratic thought curiously converge) denounced the efforts of the medical profession to monopolize the art of healing. These efforts, it should be noted, reflected not only a growing sense of professionalism (in medicine as in law, academic life, and other callings) but the same drive for efficiency, rationality, and uniform standards that was being pressed by the business community. Just as large corporations tried to eliminate "unfair trade practices" (for instance, the adulteration of meat), so the medical profession tried to eliminate what it regarded as quackery. The bureaucratization of business had its counterpart in the bureaucratization of knowledge. Populists opposed both—the "medical monopoly" as well as the trusts. Thus William James, like Flower, defended "medical freedom" and the need for "psychic research."

Flower saw the link between his crusade for medical freedom, his anti-Catholicism, and his opposition to the business corporation as follows: "Law-bulwarked privilege, possessing monopoly power, has always fattened off of productive industry. . . . But baleful as is the influence of privilege in the realm of commercial activity, the evil dwarfs into insignificance when compared with its influence in fields that are largely speculative or theoretical; for here, while exerting the same improverishing and demoralizing effects that mark it in the domain of material life, it encroaches on things intimately personal. Religion and the healing art afford two striking historic illustrations of this fact."[4] The conflict between productive industry and parasitic non-industry could thus be seen to run through all

[4] B. O. Flower: *Progressive Men, Women and Movements of the Past Twenty-Five Years* (Boston: The New Arena; 1914), p. 299.

endeavor, justifying a radicalism that went beyond strictly economic issues. Ignatius Donnelly, another populist spokesman, engaged simultaneously in radical politics and in unconventional works of scholarship on the Baconian theory of Shakespeare and the lost island of Atlantis in which the non-specialist openly defied the organized community of scholarship. Donnelly's *Atlantis: The Antediluvian World* was, in effect, an attack on the knowledge trust conceived in the same spirit that animated Flower's denunciations of the medical monopoly. When scholars rejected it, Donnelly complained that an outsider with a new idea could not get a hearing among American scholars unless the idea had "the brand of foreign approval." "What we call 'Science' in this country," he raged, "is upheld by a congeries of schoolmasters repeating what someone else has told them."[5]

Donnelly and Flower represented a type of Populist attracted to a wide variety of reformist causes. The People's party also contained a purely agrarian element, led by men like James B. Weaver, the party's presidential candidate in 1892, who interpreted the struggle of productive against parasitic labor almost exclusively as a struggle of the American farmer against the "interests"—the railroads and the goldbugs. The Populists' decision to fuse with the Democrats in 1896 behind Bryan and free silver dictated the abandonment of the other reforms for which the party had

---

[5] Martin Ridge: *Ignatius Donnelly* (Chicago: University of Chicago Press; 1962), pp. 209–10. After completing his study of Shakespeare, *The Great Cryptogram*, Donnelly wrote in his diary: "A good many people believe that the proper occupation for a person of Irish blood is digging a ditch or flourishing a shilela. They are presumed to know nothing about literature & to ultimately lack those qualities of patience & perseverance which are held to be the birthright of the Anglo-Saxon. I think I have done something to dispel that prejudice." (Ibid., p. 232)

once stood. For this reason men like Donnelly, Lloyd, and Watson, together with a majority of the party, opposed fusion. In the future politics of agrarianism, however, it was the minority point of view that shaped the course of events. Fusion led to the disintegration of populism and the emergence of a very different kind of agrarian politics, the politics of the farm bloc. The People's party gave way to the Farm Bureau Federation, which subsequently achieved what populism had failed to achieve (if indeed the Populists had even wished to achieve it)—that is, official recognition of farmers as a special interest entitled to the special protection of the parity system, which has now become a permanent fixture of the welfare state.[6] The farmers achieved this position, however, at the price of the generalized democratic enthusiasm, the demand for the wholesale reformation of a corrupt society, which had originally inspired the Populist movement. "The people are demoralized," the Populists cried in their platform of 1892. Such considerations could not have been more remote from the aims and objectives of the Farm Bureau Federation.

In short, agrarian discontent gradually parted company with reform. The same thing happened to the labor movement. The Knights of Labor, which flourished in the 1880's, bore the same relation to the labor movement as populism to agrarian radicalism. The culmination of an older tradition, it fell victim to attacks within and without and gave way to a narrower and more "businesslike" concept of what a labor movement ought to be.

The Knights, like the Populists, were broadly reformist. Their head, Terence V. Powderley, busied himself with a whole variety of reforms, of which the labor movement was

[6] On the decline of agrarian radicalism and the emergence of agrarian interest-group politics, see Richard Hofstadter: *The Age of Reform* (New York: Alfred A. Knopf; 1955), Ch. iii.

only one, and in his mind not necessarily the most important. At times he thought that temperance was the "main issue." At other times he believed that the "all-absorbing question of the hour is the land question."[7] Powderly was an odd blend of radicalism and timidity. He was radical in holding out for a comprehensive rather than a piecemeal reform of society, in his attack on economic individualism and on the morally corrupting effects of capitalism, and in his underlying vision of a cooperative society. On the other hand, his aversion to strikes, his curious shrinking from the consequences of the Knights' very successes, and his general failure to assert leadership when it was most needed, were more than temperamental failings; they were the failings of the labor movement in general, which drew back from the conflicts to which its own ideology logically led.

The opponents of the Knights appealed very persuasively to these weaknesses. The AFL, while repudiating not only theories of class enmity but the concept of "one big union," of which the Knights of Labor was an early expression, nevertheless used forcible and even violent action in the interests of the select group of tradesmen it chose to represent. But in every other respect Samuel Gompers's "business unionism" represented a strategic retreat from the reformism of the Knights. It was exclusive where the Knights were inclusive, apolitical where the Knights were political, "practical" where the Knights were moral. Avoiding "entangling alliances with intellectuals," Gompers turned the AFL into a pressure group which attempted to win for a minority of workers—skilled, native workers in the older trades—the same kind of recognition the Farm Bureau Federation sought for a minority of farmers. "The trade unions," he said, "are the business organizations of the

[7] Norman Ware: *The Labor Movement in the United States* (New York: D. Appleton; 1929), pp. 89, 88.

wage-earners, to attend to the business of the wage-earners."[8] The difficulty with which even this modest conception of the labor movement was finally realized should not obscure the main point, that here again, what took place was a splitting-off of the reform impulse from the particular clusters of interests that originally lay behind it—in this case, a divorce between labor and reform.

[III]

The civil rights movement underwent a similar change in the late nineteenth century. During Reconstruction, Negro leaders in the South, together with their abolitionist allies, tried to realize a program of social and economic reform through political action. The next generation of Negro leaders, under Booker T. Washington, engineered a retreat from reform in favor of the same "practical," immediate, and seemingly more realistic objectives toward which Gompers had steered the main body of the labor movement. Like Gompers, Washington spoke the language of the American business culture and tried to assure businessmen that recognition of the rights of minorities posed no threat to the status quo. In this way he was able to win business support for Negro education in the South. But his program deliberately sacrificed the reformist goals to which black leadership during Reconstruction had been committed. Under Washington, Negroes now renounced, with professions of horror, not only the claim to "social equality" but the vote.

The results of Washington's efforts were by no means

---

[8] Quoted in Carl N. Degler: *Out of Our Past* (New York: Harper & Bros.; 1959), p. 267.

negligible. Insofar as they contributed to the growth of a semiseparate Negro subculture in the South, they laid the groundwork for the re-emergence of the Southern civil rights movement in the 1950's.[9] More immediately, Washington's leadership helped to save the black community in the South from the full effects of the savage racist reaction that took place around the turn of the century. At that time there were people in the South who were advocating the total suppression of the Negroes' cultural personality; advocating, in effect, the complete reduction of Negroes to work animals. Some people went even further and preached open aggression against the Negro "beast," and the sudden rise in lynchings testified to the prevalence of these feelings. So rapidly had race relations deteriorated since Reconstruction that the great question was no longer whether Negroes should be allowed to vote but whether they should be allowed to live; not whether they should be educated in the same schools as white children but whether they should go to school at all. In Mississippi, James K. Vardaman frankly proposed to do away with Negro education altogether. Washington's compromises made it possible for Southern progressives to cite the moderation of Negro leadership in support of their contention—bold enough in the context of the times—that the rights of Negroes ought not to be totally obliterated.[1]

In the North, however, the type of Negro leadership personified in some ways by Booker T. Washington had a very different effect. Here the emphasis on moderation, on limited goals, and on winning the support of white businessmen, far from encouraging the development of a separate

---

[9] See below, pp. 122 ff.

[1] See, for example, Edgar Gardner Murphy: *Problems of the Present South* (New York: Macmillan; 1904) and *The Basis of Ascendancy* (New York: Longmans, Green; 1909).

black culture (which would have been a very desirable thing), encouraged the "integration" of Negro leaders—politicians, journalists, and clergymen—into the white middle class. Particularly after the collapse of black nationalism in the twenties, spokesmen for the ghetto tended increasingly to take on the values of the surrounding culture. They identified themselves with America's wars, with its domestic policies, and with much of its rhetoric of equality and opportunity. The typical leader of the Northern ghetto began to acquire the characteristics of the "professional" representative of stigmatized groups, described by Erving Goffman in another connection as a man who does not so much speak for the stigmatized as *to* the stigmatized on behalf of "normal" society.

"In making a profession of their stigma," Goffman writes, "native leaders are obliged to have dealings with representatives of other categories, and so find themselves breaking out of the closed circle of their kind. Instead of leaning on their crutch, they get to play golf with it, ceasing, in terms of social participation, to be representative of the people they represent." It is these leaders who define, for the groups they no longer represent but whom they lead in the absence of other leadership, the nature of what society regards as a "good adjustment" to blindness, crippling injury, humiliating bodily deformity—or to the pain of being black in a white society. A "good adjustment" to these misfortunes requires "that the stigmatized individual cheerfully and unself-consciously accept himself as essentially the same as normals, while at the same time he voluntarily withholds himself from those situations in which normals would find it difficult to give lip service to their similar acceptance of him." The purpose of such an implicit code of behavior governing relations between normal people and the stigmatized, and communicated to the latter through the intermediary of their "professional" representatives, is to perpetuate the illusion of equality without its substance.

"The stigmatized individual is asked to act so as to imply neither that his burden is heavy nor that bearing it has made him different from us; at the same time he must keep himself at that remove from us which ensures our painlessly being able to confirm this belief about him. . . . So deeply, then, must he be caught up in the attitude to the self that is defined as normal in our society, so thoroughly must he be a part of this definition, that he can perform this self in a faultless manner to an edgy audience that is half-watching him in terms of another show. He can even be led to join with normals in suggesting to the discontented among his own that the slights they sense are imagined slights. . . . And in truth he will have accepted a self for himself; but this self is, as it necessarily must be, a resident alien, a voice of the group that speaks for and through him."[2]

Thanks to the success with which "professional Negroes"

[2] Erving Goffman: *Stigma: Notes on the Management of Spoiled Identity* (Englewood Cliffs: Prentice-Hall; 1963), pp. 27, 121, 123. Goffman deliberately excludes the race problem from his analysis of "spoiled identity," on the grounds that established minorities do not provide the best objects for an analysis of the delicate mechanisms surrounding the management of stigma. "Sociologically, the central issue concerning these groups is their place in the social structure; the contingencies these persons encounter in face-to-face interaction is only one part of the problem, and something that cannot itself be fully understood without reference to the history, the political development, and the current policies of the group." (Ibid., p. 127) At the same time an understanding of face-to-face relationships drawn from a quite different perspective throws unexpected light on certain aspects of race relations—notably on the role of "professionals." As Goffman notes with his usual acuity, traditional fields of study such as race relations are areas "to which one should apply several perspectives"; and "the development of any one of these coherent analytic perspectives is not likely to come from those who restrict their interest exclusively to one substantive area." (Ibid., p. 147).

convinced their constituents that the way to acceptance lay in this kind of acquiescence to the myth of equality, Northern whites lived for years in the illusion that steady progress toward justice was being made; black people never told them otherwise. On Negroes themselves, meanwhile, the constant pretense of having been accepted, combined with the reality of rejection, amounted to "a recipe," as Kardiner and Ovesey wrote some years ago in their study of the Negro personality, "for perpetual self-hatred, frustration, and for tying one's life to unattainable goals. . . . The acceptance of the white ideal has acted on the Negro as a slow but cumulative and fatal psychological poison."[3]

The waning of Negro radicalism, in some ways running parallel to the waning of agrarian and working-class radicalism, offers a perspective from which to criticize the conventional explanation that the agrarian and labor movements subsided because they won the objectives for which they had been working. What happened in all of these cases, as we can see with particular clarity in the case of the northern Negro, was that the objectives themselves were

---

[3] Abram Kardiner and Lionel Ovesey: *The Mark of Oppression* (Cleveland: Meridian Books; 1962 [New York, 1951]), p. 310. The same point emerges from the more recent study, William H. Grier and Price M. Cobbs: *Black Rage* (New York: Basic Books; 1968). A stigmatized group, it should be noted, does not necessarily "accept the white ideal." That is, it does not necessarily accept the evaluation of itself as stigmatized. As Goffman notes, some groups, for example "Mennonites, Gypsies, shameless scoundrels, and very orthodox Jews," think of outsiders as "the ones who are not quite human"; they bear a stigma, in the eyes of the dominant group, but do "not seem to be impressed or repentant about doing so." (*Stigma,* p. 6) This reaction, however, presupposes that the group has developed a strong and supportive subculture of its own. The absence of such a culture in the Northern black ghetto, accordingly, must be seen as one of the most important determinants of the black man's situation. See below, pp. 123 ff.

redefined in such a way as to make their realization possible without any basic modification of American institutions. In each case an exploited group won for itself a kind of toleration which at least permitted it to exist, and which in the case of farmers and workers eventually brought material as well as symbolic concessions. But these successes, such as they were, entailed the sacrifice of democratic values the defense of which, in the beginning, had been these movements' whole reason for being. Not only did former radicals restrict their objectives to what now seemed "practical," not only did they take on the rhetoric and values of the business culture which they had formerly condemned, but they also restricted their membership, quite deliberately, to the more affluent and successful among their followers—the agrarians by excluding tenants, sharecroppers, and migratory workers; the AFL by excluding immigrants, Negroes, and unskilled workers in general; and the Negroes themselves by holding up the "good Negro," agreeably middle-class and conservative in his habits and outlook, as the ideal representative of the race. So pervasive was the discriminatory atmosphere within movements formerly dissident and democratic that even W. E. B. DuBois, later one of the architects of black nationalism, argued for a time that the Negro elite, the "talented tenth," ought to be considered the spearhead of the drive toward integration and acceptance.

[IV]

The collapse of feminism, like the collapse of other popular radicalisms, has usually been attributed to the achievement of the goals in question, in this case woman suffrage. Nineteenth century feminists, however, wanted much more than the suffrage. They were more interested in social than in political questions. In their view, the relations between men and women had been corrupted by the glorification of female sexuality and the subordination of other aspects of womanhood to the power of sexual attraction. The universal expectation that woman's principal function in life was to please men made marriage itself, according to the feminists, a sort of higher prostitution. The "respectable" woman, instead of selling herself to a series of casual visitors, sold herself once and for all to the highest bidder for her hand, in return for a lifetime of leisure and security. The economic "parasitism" of women, the feminists argued, was both cause and consequence of this system; and economic self-sufficiency, therefore—not the ballot—appeared to them to be the only means by which the system could be fundamentally changed.[4] The feminists proposed to do for women what other democrats were trying to do for society in general: to eliminate the dependence of certain kinds of people on their "superiors" and to bring about a situation in which every individual would be able to stand, economically and therefore morally, on his own feet. The idea of self-reliance was the moral heart of early feminism.

Toward the end of the nineteenth century the feminist movement experienced a decisive change of character. Wealthy women of leisure, like Alva Vanderbilt—women not previously noted for the breadth of their sympathies— came to exercise a preponderant influence. For these women, votes for women had become a single-minded obsession, divorced from every other objective. In pursuit of the ballot the suffragists occasionally resorted (as in England) to radical

[4] For these arguments see, for example, Charlotte Perkins Stetson [Gilman]: *Women and Economics* (Boston: Small, Maynard & Co.; 1900).

forms of agitation, but the important point is that they compromised again and again with the democratic principles for which they claimed to speak. The appeal to self-reliance gave way to the argument that votes for women would counteract the bad effects of the immigrant and Negro vote. In order to appease the emerging suffrage movement in the South, Northern suffragists began to couple the demand for women suffrage with proposals for literacy and even property tests designed to disfranchise undesirable elements of the population. Susan B. Anthony had urged her colleagues to "give your heaviest raps on the head of every Nabob—man or woman—who does injustice to a human being—for the crime! of color or sex!!" "But, by the last decade of the nineteenth century," Aileen Kraditor writes, "woman suffrage had become respectable, and women who held orthodox opinions on every other issue could now join a suffrage organization without fear of ostracism."[5] Feminism died, not because it accomplished what it set out to accomplish, but because it lost sight of the conditions which had called it into being.

In the end, women won the vote and achieved semi-official status as an organized interest. They owed this position more to their growing influence as consumers than to their influence as voters; nor has their position as an official minority been very clearly defined. Nevertheless one can discern here the same patterns of official deference—recognition of women as a minority in good standing—that one observes, more clearly, in the cases already discussed. The media, for example, ritually respect the "woman's point of view." A representative panel of experts, of the

[5] Aileen S. Kraditor: *The Ideas of the Woman Suffrage Movement* (New York: Columbia University Press; 1965), pp. 78, 85.

kind which publicly debate the two sides to every non-question, for the edification of serious people for whom politics presents itself as a series of "issues," may include a woman as well as a Negro. Patriotic and military organizations maintain "women's divisions." This is hardly the kind of equality the early feminists had in mind, but the new arrangements created the illusion, at least, of equality.

The "emancipation" of women, such as it was, came about for reasons having little to do with the original goals of the feminist movement. The suffrage movement won its first triumphs in the western states not because the West was unusually receptive to radical ideas but because the movement had shuffled off whatever radical ideas it may once have had and now associated itself with the civilizing mission of women, with civilization as represented by Aunt Polly—the civilization from which Huckleberry Finns have always found it necessary to light out. Woman suffrage in the West, far from springing from frontier conditions, as many historians have supposed, came about after the frontier stage had already passed and was part of an effort, in which women were prominently involved, precisely to subvert frontier conditions and to re-establish order and refinement.[6] Here as elsewhere the feminist movement gradually departed from its earlier egalitarianism and embraced prohibition, racism, and opposition to immigration. Meanwhile technological changes and improvements in medicine gradually freed women from unrelieved domesticity, excessive child-bearing, and the extreme sexual reserve which a fear of "consequences," together with other influences peculiar to the Victorian period, imposed. None of these changes struck at the confusion of sex with power—the use

[6] Alan P. Grimes: *The Puritan Ethic and Woman Suffrage* (New York: Oxford University Press; 1966).

of sexuality as a weapon in the war between the sexes—
which feminism at its most radical had attacked; nor did
they even make it possible for women to compete more
effectively for jobs. They merely gave women time to be
ladies.[7]

[V]

The process we have been discussing has created a society characterized by a high degree of uniformity, which
nevertheless lacks the cohesiveness and sense of shared experience that distinguish a truly integrated community from
an atomistic society. The apparently successful assimilation
of the social and cultural minorities which in the nineteenth
century gave to American society an appearance of extreme
disorder has led some writers to assert that a reintegration
has taken place and that the contemporary social order, in
this respect, more nearly resembles the cohesive society of
the preindustrial epoch than it resembles the anarchic individualism of the nineteenth century.[8] This view, however,
is hard to reconcile with the pervasive *anomie* of the contemporary world. The United States of the mid-twentieth
century might better be described as an empire than as a
community. The state deals with domestic minorities
through their official representatives, in much the same way
that it deals with client states abroad. These representatives,

[7] For further reflections on the decline of feminism and the "eman-
cipation" of women see my article: "Emancipated Women," *New
York Review of Books,* July 13, 1967, pp. 28–32; also J. A. and Olive
Banks: *Feminism and Family Planning in Victorian England* (New
York: Schocken Books; 1964).

[8] Rowland Berthoff: "The American Social Order: A Conservative
Hypothesis," *American Historical Review,* April 1960, pp. 495–514.

native chieftains, enjoy various pleasures and privileges; they themselves, as a result, are sufficiently integrated into the imperial order to perceive their function to be not so much to present the view of their constituents as to mediate between them and the state—by no means the same thing. Their interests lie in resolving and preventing conflicts rather than in carrying them to a successful conclusion. Their constituents, in turn, sustain these leaders in office not because their leadership is particularly effective in satisfying the material needs of the people they are supposed to represent (although in some cases undeniable improvements have taken place) but because identification with these spokesmen, who have risen from the ranks of a minority to prominence and prestige, provides vicarious and symbolic satisfactions; and because, in any case, the hierarchical and undemocratic structure of the organizations in question effectively prevents changes in leadership. Thus Jimmy Hoffa continues to head the Teamsters' Union, and the first ward of Chicago faithfully returns William L. Dawson to the House of Representatives, even though these leaders have so completely identified themselves with the establishment that they are incapable of seeing things from any but the official point of view.

Even if the system of interest-group politics functioned as it is supposed to function, even if the official minority spokesmen really represented the interests of their constituents, those interests have come to be so narrowly defined, as we have seen, that they imply very little criticism of the status quo. No matter how one looks at the matter, the conclusion is inescapable that constituted leaders of social, cultural, and ethnic minorities have ceased to function as critics of American society.

The drying-up of traditional sources of dissent helps to explain why democratic values show so little vitality in contemporary society. It also makes it easier to understand the peculiar rigidity which until recently has characterized the postindustrial order. Appeals to "get America moving again," even if they are sincere, make no impression on the political system: each administration, whatever its predilections, whatever its ostensible peculiarities, ends by perpetuating the already bankrupt policies of its predecessors. The explanation of this political stagnation lies neither in the "conservatism" of certain politicians—for "liberals" have shown themselves to be equally conservative—nor, in itself, in the persistence of cold-war strategies beyond their usefulness. It is true that outmoded ideas shape national policies, but the important point is that this condition has institutional roots. The structure of American society makes it almost impossible for criticism of existing policies to become part of political discourse. The language of American politics increasingly resembles an Orwellian monologue.

Early students of the brave new world—which is unmistakably the world we now live in—made the mistake of thinking that a monolithic society is impervious to change. But rigidity is not the same thing as stability. Indeed the rigidity of the American system has become itself a source of extreme instability. It has led the country to the verge of a crisis, the outlines of which are beginning to emerge—too late, it may be, to allow anyone to avert it. The cities, where most of the people live, have become almost uninhabitable, and their problems increasingly appear insoluble within the conventional framework. Ghettos of misery and deprivation, the cities smolder until one of them bursts into fire: today Watts and Newark, tomorrow some other "pocket of poverty." Riots, with the deep and unqualified hatreds that call them into being, point to a disturbing fact: there are vast numbers of people in the United States whom a society that has tried to organize everything has signally failed to organize. Organization, in fact, was achieved precisely by eliminating in advance all who could not be organized with a minimum of effort—immigrants, Negroes, sharecroppers, hillbillies; the "culturally deprived." Poverty has not been eliminated, it has merely been concealed. Because they are both "invisible" and voiceless, the millions of poor have no way of making their presence felt except by violence; but precisely because they are leaderless and unorganized, violence, once it erupts, cannot be directed by radicals toward political objectives. Meanwhile the public safety seems to many Americans to require increasingly repressive measures on the part of a state whose powers have already dangerously expanded, and which finds itself inextricably involved in similar police actions abroad.

These internal and foreign police actions, demanding by their very nature brutal repression on an unprecedented scale, breed a new class of men, deeply attached at once to violence and to "order," contemptuous of bourgeois flabbiness, contemptuous of democracy, openly fascist in their sympathies. It is these elements, if the history of the recent past is any indication, which more and more come to be seen—as they see themselves—as guardians of order and safety at home as well as in the colonies. A government faced with insuperable difficulties of every kind, a government that has already ceased in any meaningful sense to govern, will find itself increasingly dependent on its imperial police, and a panicky population will put no obstacles in the way of this dependence. For the citizens fear not only the dark, unpredictable violence of the poor but the inscrutable sullenness of their own children, the other group of rioters who have risen up to haunt respectable people. The radical dissociation of the young from the adult world is no mere political fashion of the moment; it is a built-in feature of societies in which the institutional links between generations have broken down. The creation of the multiversity has rendered the campus politically volatile. Thus good people need to protect themselves not only against the rioters of Watts but against the rioters of San Francisco State and Columbia, their own flesh and blood, ranged against their elders in their bewildering defiance, their garb of poverty voluntarily assumed, and their incomprehensible rhetoric of dissaffection.

Under these circumstances the only alternative to some form of despotism, benevolent or openly terroristic, is a reawakening of the democratic instinct in middle-class Americans who have no material need to revolt but who are becoming conscious of the degree to which they too are corrupted, degraded, and victimized by the very arrangements that have made possible their unprecedented prosperity. This potential too exists in our society, along with others. At present it takes the form of a pervasive self-contempt in the more literate and sophisticated portion of the nation, a masochistic relish in the denunciations of itself (which its "black" comedians are eager to furnish on demand) as empty, conformist, sexually repressed, and dead to feeling. But the institutional means by which this sterile self-contempt—as empty, in itself, as the emptiness against which it is directed—can be translated into an ethical sense, a sense of injustice, a reawakened sense of the indignities and humiliations which men have permitted themselves to accept as normal, inevitable, proper, and moral—these institutions, it appears, have yet to be forged.

THE COLLAPSE
OF SOCIALISM
AND THE ISOLATION
OF THE INTELLECTUALS

I N THE YEARS IMMEDIATELY PRECEDING THE FIRST WORLD War, the socialist movement laid down deep roots in the United States, in spite of many obstacles. James Weinstein, in a brilliant study of the Socialist party that will alter many of the prevailing assumptions about American radicalism, shows that at its numerical peak in 1912, the party had 118,000 members well distributed throughout the country. It claimed 323 English- and foreign-language publications with a total circulation probably in excess of two million. The largest of the Socialist newspapers, *The Appeal to Reason* of Girard, Kansas, had a weekly circulation of 761,747. In 1912, the year Eugene V. Debs polled six per cent of the Presidential vote, Socialists held 1,200 offices in 340 cities, including 79 mayors in 24 states. As late as 1918, they elected 32 state legislators. In 1916, they elected Meyer London to Congress and made important gains in the municipal elections of several large cities.[1]

In sharp contrast to later radical organizations, the Socialist party was broad enough to include many different tendencies and points of view; nor did these harden into factions or hostile sects. Contrary to an accepted view of prewar socialism as narrow and marginal—a view, according

[1] James Weinstein: *The Decline of Socialism in America, 1912–1925* (New York: Monthly Review Press; 1967), pp. 27, 84–5, 93, 103, 115.

to Weinstein, that reads back into an earlier period the characteristics of American radicalism in the late twenties and thirties—the party was inclusive, nonsectarian, and given to "searching and open debate." Another cliché about socialism is that the party declined rapidly after 1912; but a close study of the evidence, Weinstein argues, discloses "a patchwork pattern [of losses and gains] which does not lend itself to generalizations."[2] In his view, neither the New Freedom nor the war destroyed the Socialist party; rather, it died from internal wounds inflicted in a series of struggles growing out of the Bolshevik revolution and the rise of a militant new left wing. Weinstein's detailed analysis of these battles, together with his reassessment of the prewar Socialist party, casts the entire history of the American Left into a new light.

The strength of the prewar party, if we are to accept Weinstein's view, lay in its ability to combine a commitment to thoroughgoing social transformation with "constructive" political action, in the party's terminology—that is, responsiveness to the needs of its constituents. Thus the Socialists cooperated with the trade union movement in its attempt to win immediate gains for workers and opposed dual unionism on the grounds that it jeopardized those gains, without on the other hand identifying itself so closely with the union movement that the party itself, as in Europe, was absorbed into the industrial system, becoming dependent on its continuation and therefore unable to dissociate itself from the catastrophes into which capitalist society was about to plunge. If the Socialist Party of America, alone among socialist organizations in the West, opposed the First World War, that was because it saw its function not as the promotion of unionism as such but as the creation of socialist

[2] Ibid., pp. 87, 115.

consciousness in the working class and its middle-class allies. On the one hand the party consistently criticized those
tendencies in American unionism which tied the unions
ever more closely to capitalism, while on the other hand it
refused to lend itself to raids on existing unions which, for
all their inadequacies, spoke for the immediate interests of
the working class. Eugene V. Debs joined the IWW when it
appeared that it would organize the unorganized and promote the growth of industrial unionism; he left it when the
IWW began to devote itself not to organizing workers
whom the trade unions had refused to organize but to winning workers away from established unions.

In the revolutionary mystique currently fashionable in
some sections of the Left, the IWW, not the Socialist party,
represents the vanguard of American radicalism.[3] It is not
hard to see why: Haywood's militancy, his advocacy of violence and sabotage, his tirades against the "scum proletariat" of "lawyers, preachers, authors, lecturers, and intellectual non-producers generally," and his view of radicalism as
a movement based on marginal people, all correspond to
the anti-intellectual proclivities of the contemporary student
left. Weinstein's study, however, argues convincingly that
"while the romantic appeal of the Wobblies has triumphed
in literature and history, as a social force the IWW did not
approach the Socialist Party in its impact on contemporary
American life."[4] Even the Communists, who joined the
IWW in denouncing the Socialists as bourgeois reformers,
eventually recognized that the Wobblies' dual unionism,
their refusal to join political movements, and their obsession with direct action were attitudes fatal to the attempt to

[3] On the question of the IWW see the exchange between Weinstein and Paul Buhle in *Radical America*, January–February 1968,
pp. 44–59.

[4] Weinstein: *The Decline of Socialism*, pp. 15n., 1.

organize a mass movement for revolutionary change. As William Z. Foster pointed out in 1921, shortly before he entered the Communist party, the Wobblies violated "the first principle of working-class solidarity" by forsaking the "real organizations of labor, based on the common economic interests" of workingmen, and forming instead "outside organizations, based upon revolutionary creed."[5] Only when the Communists adopted this position regarding the IWW—in other words, the Socialist position, which they had earlier opposed—did respected unionists like Foster join the party.

[II]

By that time the Socialists themselves had been fatally weakened by the revolt of their own left wing, and could derive little comfort from the Communists' belated acknowledgement of the superiority of certain Socialist principles. The immediate effect of the war and the Russian revolution, Weinstein shows, had been to move "the Socialist party's center of gravity leftward, and . . . to reduce earlier hostilities" within the party.[6] The left and right wings joined in condemning the war. Events in Russia, however, led some left-wing Socialists to believe that the Bolsheviks' success could be duplicated in America and thus revived lingering suspicions of the moderate leadership of Victor Berger and Morris Hillquit, who argued that the war had "strengthened capitalism, reaction and *treason* within the *working class*," making the prospects for immediate revolution even bleaker than before. "While we can

[5] Ibid., p. 268.
[6] Ibid., p. 177.

learn from [the Bolsheviks]," Berger wrote, "we cannot transfer Russia to America."[7] The new left wing—Louis Fraina, Louis Boudin, Charles E. Ruthenberg, and Ludwig Lore, among others—disagreed.

The growing militance of the IWW-oriented American Left coincided with the increasing influence of the foreign-language federations, which made up only thirty-five per cent of the Socialist party membership in 1917 but which by 1919 had grown to fifty-three per cent of the party—a reflection of wartime losses suffered by the Socialists in the West and South and of the growth of socialist feeling among immigrant workers in the industrial cities of the North. The foreign-language federations, in their preoccupation with European events, convinced themselves that the Socialist party had played the same role in American politics as the social democratic parties in Europe—in Fraina's words, "had become part of the governing system of things, indirectly its ally and protector."[8] This analysis made some sense in Europe, where the social democrats had supported the war and now opposed the Bolsheviks (though even there it rested on the fundamentally erroneous premise that world revolution was imminent); but its application to the United States showed nothing but ignorance of American conditions. As Weinstein points out, "in the American Party, there were virtually no right wingers in the European sense: i.e., supporters of the war and of the postwar attacks on the Soviet Republic. But . . . the left wing converted the European reality into a universal formula. If the facts did not fit the formula, in the United States, so much the worse for the facts."[9]

[7] Ibid., p. 207.
[8] Ibid., p. 190.
[9] Ibid., p. 193.

Convinced that splitting the Socialist party was the necessary prelude to revolution, the new left wing, led by Nicholas I. Hourwich and Santeri Nuorteva of the Russian Language Federation together with their American allies, prepared either to capture the party or to desert it. The moderates responded by expelling the dissidents, who themselves split into hostile factions, one dominated by the Russian Federation, more Leninist than the Leninists, and the other by American left-wingers carrying on the dualunionist, antipolitical traditions of the IWW. In September 1919 the former organized the Communist party and the latter the Communist Labor party. (In 1921 the Comintern ordered them merged.) The effect of these events, not only on the Socialist party but on American radicalism in general, was immediately reflected in the decline of membership. Early in 1919 the Socialist party still contained 109,000 members; after the split the three parties together had a membership of only 36,000.[1] Nor was this all. "Socialist influence in the labor movement, except for pockets in the garment trades, was all but destroyed by the split, and the socialist press . . . was permanently debilitated. In the decade that followed the split, the lines drawn in 1919 were erected into walls, and the movement became one of hostile and warring sects."[2] By the middle twenties American radicalism had acquired the characteristics it has retained until the present day: sectarianism, marginality, and alienation from American life.

The history of white radicalism in the twentieth century, as it emerges from Weinstein's history of the decline of socialism, remarkably resembles, in essential respects, the his-

---

[1] Ibid., p. 232; see also Theodore Draper: *The Roots of American Communism* (New York: Viking Press; 1957), p. 207.

[2] Weinstein: *The Decline of Socialism,* pp. 232–3.

tory of black radicalism as analyzed by Harold Cruse in *The Crisis of the Negro Intellectual*.[3] Together these works represent the beginnings of a new understanding not only of radicalism but of the nature of American society, which differs in critical ways from the European societies on which so much of the radical tradition has unfortunately been based. In both cases, the early years of the twentieth century saw impressive and partially successful attempts to create a mass-based, indigenous radicalism among dis-affected groups—socialism among the working-class poor and among middle-class intellectuals, black nationalism in the Negro ghetto. Had these efforts persisted, they might eventually have converged, each movement enriching and strengthening the other. To a dialogue between socialists and black nationalists, of the kind that should have taken place forty years ago, the black nationalists would have contributed an awareness of the need to shape socialism to the peculiar requirements of American ethnic-group plural-ism, while the socialists would have been able to show that "self-determination for the ghetto" logically led not to a separate black capitalism but to the socialization and decen-tralization of the entire economy.[4] Instead both movements

[3] (New York: William Morrow; 1967). For a full discussion of this work see below, pp. 154 ff.

[4] On some radical implications of black nationalism see Eugene D. Genovese: "The Legacy of Slavery and the Roots of Black National-ism," *Studies on the Left,* November–December 1966, p. 23: "The demands of the black community will increasingly swing away from the traditional appeal to federal power and toward the assertion of local and regional autonomy. . . . The naive fascination of leftists for centralized power has, since the 1930's, greatly strengthened [the tendency toward state paternalism, which Genovese thinks is also reflected in the integrationist approach to the race issue, with its almost exclusive reliance on state action]. With such labels as 'pro-gressive' and even 'socialist,' corporate liberalism has been building what William Appleman Williams has aptly called a nonterroristic

simultaneously underwent a process of Europeanization which set in directly after the Bolshevik revolution. Black nationalism gave way to the "revolutionary solution" of the Communists—"a fighting alliance of the Negro masses and white workers" to organize the working class and create a proletarian culture.[5] The Socialist party suffered a similar fate. Instead of perfecting their analysis of American conditions and of continuing to present alternatives in a way that would be appropriate to those conditions the new militants, both white and black, imposed on their movements an ideology drawn from European experience and tied organizationally to the fluctuating political requirements of the Soviet Union. The tremendous prestige of the Russian revolution overrode the opposition even of those who supported the revolution but who argued that it was not necessarily the best guide to events in America. The new militants enjoyed the inestimable advantage of their association with what appeared to be a world-wide revolutionary wave, and even when the immediate hope of revolution receded, the Soviet Union continued for a long time to command an "almost mystical prestige."[6] In the years immediately fol-

---

totalitarian society. Yet American socialism has never even posed a theoretical alternative. When Professor Williams called for a program of regional and local reassertion and opposition to centralization, he was dismissed by most radicals as a Utopian of doubtful mental competence. We may now rephrase his question: How do we propose to support an increasingly nationalistic black radicalism, with its demands for local hegemony, unless we have an ideology and program of opposition to the centralization of state power?" In a rejoinder to Genovese (ibid., p. 34), Herbert Aptheker, the leading Communist authority on black history, predictably attacks black nationalism and rather confusingly adds: "I join in Genovese's appeal for enhanced power in localities. I do not see this in any way, however, as contrary to enhancing power nationally."

[5] Cruse: *The Crisis of the Negro Intellectual*, p. 143.
[6] Weinstein: *The Decline of Socialism*, p. 209.

lowing the revolution, moreover, the Kremlin's call for the immediate overthrow of capitalism coincided with and reinforced the romantic, anarchistic tendencies within American radicalism, undermining those who believed in the patient work of organization.[7] The militant left wing of American radicalism, as the Socialist Ralph Korngold pointed out in 1919, appealed to "revolutionary romanticists" who were "tired of voting" and "tired of teaching the masses how to vote," and who proposed to make a revolution, "as far as anyone is able to make out," by "the general strike, supplemented by general rioting."[8] The euphoria of 1919 was quickly dissipated, but by that time the radical movement had been split beyond repair.

[III]

The destruction of socialism in the United States had enduring consequences for American radicalism. The most important, perhaps, was the isolation of intellectuals from the rest of society. Marxian theory, no longer joined to a mass movement, became almost entirely a preoccupation of literary intellectuals attracted to Marxism not as a social theory but, as T. B. Bottomore points out in his *Critics of Society,* principally as a means of continuing "in another fashion, that alienation from American society which had begun towards the end of the nineteenth century."[9] Bot-

---

[7] The mood of 1919 was not unlike that of 1968, except that the glamour of the Communists has now been transferred to the advocates of guerrilla warfare, as the center of the world revolution shifts from Moscow to Peking and Hanoi.

[8] Weinstein: *The Decline of Socialism,* p. 205.

[9] T. B. Bottomore: *Critics of Society: Radical Thought in North America* (New York: Pantheon Books; 1968), p. 39.

tomore's essay, which attempts to demonstrate and to explain the reasons for the poverty of social criticism in the United States, makes one aware of the degree to which American Marxism has served as a form of cultural protest and withdrawal rather than as a method of social analysis. Even in the thirties, an allegedly Marxist period of American intellectual life, Marxism was not widely accepted; its influence even on "Marxists" was superficial; and "there was not created any significant body of Marxist social thought applied directly to American society and culture."[1] The major works of social criticism in the 1930's, Bottomore reminds us—for example, Berle and Means's *The Modern Corporation and Private Property*—were not Marxist; while the writings of Veblen, which in other countries have been absorbed into a socialist tradition of thought, became associated with theories of the "managerial revolution" many of which ended up by giving implicit support to the status quo."[2] Socialist theory, meanwhile, remained "an affair of small political sects" among "socially isolated intellectuals."[3]

If social theory in the United States has been until recently "a somewhat weakly growth," the chief reason for this, Bottomore argues, lies in the lack of strong links between theory and political action. "The absence of a broad radical movement . . . and the inability to work out an effective social theory [are] related."[4] There is a "two-way intellectual traffic," according to Bottomore, between criticism and politics. "The social movements produce new ideas about their problems and about their possible solu-

[1] Ibid., pp. 37–46.
[2] For some recent variations on the managerial theory of American society see below, pp. 194 ff.
[3] Bottomore: *Critics of Society,* pp. 41, 46.
[4] Ibid., pp. 137, 45.

tions, while the critics seek to interpret on a broader scale the meaning of the social conflicts in which the movements are involved."[5] This interchange between action and theory, and more broadly between politics and culture, was just beginning to bear results in the early years of this century, which produced not only the "new history," the beginnings of a critical sociology, and brilliant theorists like Veblen, but the artistic awakenings in Greenwich Village and Harlem. "During this time, the socialists, the trade unions, . . . the pragmatists, the muckrakers, the new generation of sociologists, seemed to be converging, and even uniting, in their criticism of American society."[6] After the war these movements split apart.

In several chapters dealing with the revival of radicalism in the sixties, Bottomore shows how social criticism still suffers from the debacle of radicalism in the early twenties. Much criticism, especially of the popular variety embodied, for instance, in the work of Vance Packard or William H. Whyte—work which under different circumstances might have been fertilized by socialist theory—remains wholly satirical. As Mencken ridiculed the "booboisie," Whyte satarizes the organization man, without, however, asking whether "conformity" is a function of organization in general or of the particular circumstance that a certain kind of organization, the business corporation, "which should be merely an instrument, has set itself up in the United States as a way of life and a source of ultimate values."[7] The popular critics, Bottomore notes, have simplified and distorted the ideas of Mills, Riesman, and Eric Fromm—and even these men, he thinks, suffer from the isolation in which

[5] Ibid., p. 88.
[6] Ibid., p. 35.
[7] Ibid., p. 84.

they work. Since the First World War, the social critic in America, deprived of the advantages of the sustained tradition of criticism that would have evolved in connection with a broad movement for radical change, tends to present his ideas "as extremely personal judgments upon the state of society." This helps to explain "the lack of agreement or even clarity about what is being attacked in present-day society and what is to replace it."[8] While the analyses of Mills and Riesman converge in some respects—as in their common concern with collectivism of opinion and styles of life—in other respects they diverge, Mills drawing on the Marxian tradition, Riesman on Freud and cultural anthropology; Mills stressing the concentration of power, Riesman its dispersal. "There is little here which resembles the coherent philosophical outlook of the pragmatists in the progressive period."[9]

Another tendency in recent social criticism is existentialist irrationalism—the one philosophy that seems to have made some impression on the New Left. Even more than the others, the popularity of this point of view betrays the association between social criticism in the United States and the intellectuals' "alienation." Even more than the others, the irrationalist critiques of modern society, ranging from New Hegelian versions of Marx to various existential social philosophies, are "undogmatic, highly personal and idiosyncratic" and therefore inadequate "to sustain effective social criticism or to bring about any radical social change."[1] The only hope of a revival of effective criticism, Bottomore thinks, is that rapid social change together with the growth

[8] Ibid., pp. 80–1.
[9] Ibid., p. 64.
[1] Ibid., pp. 130, 99.

of radical movements will generate a collective effort among critics and scholars to take up the great themes of the nineteenth century where they were abandoned in the twenties and to use them as theoretical guides to the present situation. In doing so they will have to ask, among other things, whether the classic tradition of social theory did not all along underestimate the importance of national, ethnic, and racial divisions. As a Canadian, Bottomore recognizes the importance of national questions in the contemporary politics of advanced countries. Americans, faced with a "national question" of their own, ought to be similarly sensitive to such issues; but European influences, moving into the vacuum left by the failure of indigenous criticism, have consistently obscured them. Here as elsewhere, early beginnings toward an American sociology, which would have incorporated the experience of American Negroes and other experiences peculiar to the United States, proved abortive.

[IV]

The collapse of radicalism after the First World War did more than impoverish social theory. It also created a cultural crisis, the effects of which began to be felt almost at once. Before the First World War, radical politics and cultural experimentation often converged. *The Masses,* in many ways the highest product of the prewar rebellion, owed its distinctive vitality to a combination of socialism and "paganism," as Max Eastman called it. Wedded to no cultural orthodoxy, genteel or revolutionary, the magazine under Eastman, Floyd Dell, and Art Young consistently upheld high standards of artistic excellence. It prided itself on being "arrogant, impertinent, in bad taste, but not vulgar."[2] And although Eastman and Dell were eager to print "revolutionary" works of art, "neither of them for a moment," as Daniel Aaron insists, "would have judged a writer by his political affiliations. The artist as artist was beyond social criticism."[3] Not until the Russian revolution did they begin to think otherwise; and even then it was impossible for men like Eastman to accept for very long the view that revolutionary writers had to subordinate their art to politics. Eventually Eastman broke with Stalinism over this and other issues—one of the first of many Americans to conclude that "instead of liberating the mind of man, the Bolshevik revolution locked it into a state's prison tighter than ever before."[4]

The Greenwich Village renaissance, which produced *The Masses'* blend of radical politics and cultural modernism, had its counterpart, a few years later, in Harlem. As in Greenwich Village, the Harlem renaissance gave rise both to artistic experimentation and to political radicalism, and to the same questions about the relationship between them. W. E. B. DuBois, in a speech on "The Criteria of Negro Art," suggested in 1926 that Negro art should play a central part in the struggle for political liberation. Organizations like the NAACP, he thought, should address themselves not only to the issue of "civil rights" but to the cultural questions raised by Langston Hughes, Claude McKay, and other spokesmen of the Harlem renaissance. "Some in this audience . . . are thinking . . .: 'How is it that an

---

[2] Daniel Aaron: *Writers on the Left: Episodes in American Literary Communism* (New York: Harcourt, Brace & World; 1961), p. 21.

[3] Ibid., p. 25.

[4] Ibid., p. 124.

organization like this, a group of radicals, . . . can turn aside to talk about Art? After all, what have we who are slaves and black to do with Art?'" The answer, DuBois said, was that art alone could capture and preserve those "flashes" of "clairvoyance," so essential to the political movement, "of what America really is. We who are dark can see America in a way that white Americans can not."[5] Only a Negro culture, he insisted, could express this vision.

Thus in Harlem the issue was not merely whether art had anything to do with politics but whether black people were to develop their own forms of expression or to continue as cultural dependents of the white community. Because the defense of art implied a defense of ethnic culture and thus ran counter to the integrationist politics then advocated by black socialists, DuBois's position was denounced even more bitterly in Harlem than the equivalent position was denounced by the new-wave militants of the white Left. A. Philip Randolph's *Messenger*—"the only Radical Negro magazine in America," as it called itself—attacked Du-Bois's "cerebration" and made it clear that "with us economics and politics take precedence to 'Music and Art.'"[6] The Harlem renaissance never developed a counterpart of *The Masses,* which might have connected political radicalism to the search for a Negro art and thereby helped to work out a position on the relation between culture and politics that would have been of great value to American radicals in general.

The Masses itself did not survive the war and the Russian revolution. Its place was taken by *The Liberator,* which

[5] Cruse: *The Crisis of the Negro Intellectual,* p. 43.

[6] Ibid., p. 41. Throughout this discussion of culture and politics, I use the word "culture" in its narrow sense, as distinguished from the broader sense in which I shall use it elsewhere; see below, pp. 124 ff.

attempted for a time to carry on the cultural traditions of its predecessor. The new left wing, however, had very little use for the "paganism" of the old *Masses,* which smacked of "estheticism." Already Mike Gold, writing in *The Liberator* in February 1921, issued a call for "proletarian art" in which he attacked *The Seven Arts,* one of the voices of the Greenwich Village awakening. No "great lusty tree," Gold wrote, could grow in "that hot-house air."[7] Subsequent articles by Gold denounced "the mad solitary priests of Dada" and other purveyors of sterile pessimism and "pure art."[8] "Since 1912," Aaron writes, "a polarizing process had been under way which divided the Bohemian from the revolutionary" and forced writers to choose between art and radical politics.[9] But this polarization had not become critical so long as American radicalism remained a broad and inclusive movement devoted, among other things, to creating a better understanding of life under the existing order—something art is supremely equipped to do. Only when the new left wing shattered the Socialist party and substituted for long-term efforts to revolutionize American consciousness a mystique of immediate revolution did art come to be suspect in radical circles. The role of artists then came to be defined as one of dutiful servants of the "revolution"—that is, propagandists for mass culture against the stale and artificial culture of the literati, as it had come to be regarded.

In the early twenties the debate about culture reached a climax in the offices of *The Liberator.* The resignation of the Negro poet Claude McKay signalled the triumph of the new Left. After coming to America from Jamaica in 1911,

[7] Aaron: *Writers on the Left,* p. 89.
[8] Ibid.
[9] Ibid., p. 91.

McKay made friends both in Harlem and in Greenwich Village literary circles. In 1921 he joined the staff of *The Liberator,* which he hoped would maintain the literary standards of *The Masses.* It soon became apparent to McKay, however, that Gold wanted *The Liberator* to become "a popular proletarian magazine, printing doggerel from lumberjacks and stevedores and true revelations of chambermaids."[1] For his part Gold accused McKay of writing poetry "wholly lacking in working-class content."[2] He blamed McKay's degeneration on Carl van Vechten, one of the early links between the Village and Harlem and a patron of the Harlem renaissance. Van Vechten, Gold believed, was "the worst friend the Negro ever had. . . . He has been the most evil influence—Gin, jazz, and sex—this is all that stirs him in our world, and he has imparted his tastes to the young Negro literateurs. He is a white literary bum, who has created a brood of Negro literary bums."[3]

McKay resigned from *The Liberator* in 1922. Thereafter the magazine came more and more to serve as an organ of "Communist puritanical puerility," in the words of Harold Cruse.[4] *The New Masses,* which succeeded *The Liberator* in 1926, was equally devoted to "proletarian realism." Gold shared the belief that the magazine should be read, as one contributor put it, "by lumberjacks, hoboes, miners, clerks, sectionhands, machinists, harvesthands, waiters—the people who should count more to us than paid scribblers. . . . Who are we afraid of?" Joseph Kalar demanded. "Of the critics? Afraid that they will say the *New Masses* prints terribly ungrammatical stuff? Hell, brother, the newsstands abound with neat

---

[1] Ibid., p. 93; Cruse: *The Crisis of the Negro Intellectual,* p. 49.
[2] Ibid.
[3] Ibid., p. 50.
[4] Ibid.

packages of grammatical offal."[5] In searching out writers with their "roots in something real," Gold explained that he hoped to organize writers "on an industrial basis" and to create a "national corps of writers" who would report and dramatize the class struggle.[6] Meanwhile he kept up a running fire against the "dull, bloodless, intellectualistic poetry" of T. S. Eliot; against Thornton Wilder, the "prophet of the genteel Christ"; against Dostoyevsky; against Proust (the "masturbator" of the middle class); and against other "politically imbecile" writers, whom he denounced in addition as "pansies."[7]

Not until the mid-thirties was the cult of proletarianism effectively challenged. In 1934 the New York John Reed Club, founded by *The New Masses* in 1926 as part of Gold's effort to create a writers' "corps," launched a new magazine, *Partisan Review*. But whereas Gold wanted the workers "not to be bored with all the fake problems of the intelligentsia," for William Phillips and Philip Rahv, the editors of the new journal, those problems had more meaning than "the sensations of the robust young man," extolled by *The New Masses* as the ideal literary subject, "[who] sees his strength sapped by the furnace's mouth."[8] Almost immediately it became obvious to Fred Miller, editor of *Blast* ("A Magazine of Proletarian Short Studies"), that Rahv and Phillips had "lost all sense of revolutionary direction."[9] In 1936, having broken not only with Communist cultural philistinism but with Stalinist politics, *Partisan Review* sus-

[5] Quoted in Aaron: *Writers on the Left*, p. 210.

[6] Ibid., p. 213.

[7] Ibid., pp. 163, 227, 239, 241.

[8] James Burkhart Gilbert: *Writers and Partisans: A History of Literary Radicalism in America* (New York: John Wiley & Sons; 1968), p. 76.

[9] Aaron: *Writers on the Left*, p. 296.

pended publication. In 1937 it resumed as an openly anti-Stalinist magazine unblushingly "intellectualist" in its cultural standards.

Partisan Review represented the most ambitious attempt since prewar Village days to fuse radical politics and cultural modernism. From the beginning it tried "to put forward the best writing then produced by the Left," in Rahv's words.[1] Attracted to communism for the same reasons that attracted other radicals of the thirties, because it seemed to represent the best hope of social change, Rahv and Phillips had also been strongly influenced by Eliot, Joyce, James, Lawrence, Yeats, Kafka, Dostoyevsky, and other architects of the modernist tradition, and by Edmund Wilson's defense of that tradition in *Axel's Castle,* published in 1931. Somewhat disconcerted by the fact that much of this literature had been written by political reactionaries, they nevertheless recognized in the modern European classics a powerful statement of the terror and pain of contemporary existence—a revelation, they rightly perceived, that was of infinitely greater value to radicals than the shallow "realism" preached by V. F. Calverton, Mike Gold, and in slightly different form by Granville Hicks.[2] "It is true," Gold sadly observed, "that the intellectual brings into the movement many of his bourgeois hangovers, but they can be controlled."[3] Rahv and Phillips, however, as James Gilbert writes, were not prepared "to bury the culture of the past."[4]

Eventually the writers and critics around *Partisan Review,* unable to sustain both their radicalism and their devotion to avant-garde culture, despaired of politics and con-

[1] Ibid., p. 297.
[2] On Hicks see ibid., pp. 354–64 and *passim*.
[3] Gilbert: *Writers and Partisans,* p. 100.
[4] Ibid., p. 115.

fined themselves to cultural criticism. For this reason it is easy to overlook their considerable contributions to American radicalism. In the first place, they exposed the brutality of Stalinism at a time when not only radicals but many liberals still looked to the Soviet Union as the hope of the world. In the second place, they contributed to the "Europeanization" of American culture, as they called it, by introducing many Americans to the central works of modern European literature. In a rather provincial country, this was surely a service.[5] Most important of all, they battled tirelessly, even after they had ceased to argue very effectively for political radicalism, not only against proletarian "realism" but against the general proposition that "radical art" should be simple, easily understood, healthy, clean, and free from "bourgeois" influences.

The issue by no means died in the thirties. In a recent article in *The Minority of One,* Maxwell Geismar used the disclosures of CIA influence among anticommunist organizations in the fifties as the occasion for an ill-tempered harangue against the "New York literary establishment," which according to Geismar is not only politically but culturally reactionary. "It was Lionel Trilling," Geismar complains, "who outlawed such writers as Dreiser [earlier "outlawed," it might be noted, by Mike Gold himself] and Anderson, and who then 'discovered' that Henry James' *Princess Casamassima* was a counter-revolutionary novel worthy of Dostoievski. (Pure nonsense, and biased political criticism of the lowest order, since Henry James knew nothing about either revolution or counter-revolution.)" Geismar goes on to warn that "it has already been decreed" by

---

[5] On the "Europeanization" of American letters see ibid., pp. 185 ff.

these same "interlocking cultural institutions" (the ones that presumably foisted both anticommunism and the James revival on an unsuspecting public) that "William Styron's *Confessions of Nat Turner,* a rich and ripe if not fruity product of the Plantation School of Southern Liberals, is to be *the* book of the year."[6] The heated denunciation of Styron's novel, coming not only from Geismar but from Herbert Aptheker, black militants, and other radicals who object to the book's allegedly unflattering picture of slave militancy, is a perfect example of neosocialist realism; the whole controversy is so reminiscent of the thirties that intervening events seem almost not to have occurred. Just as the proletarian school of the thirties sought to dignify the workingman, the new-style socialist realists of the sixties and their historiographical counterparts in the field of Negro history insist that radical artists and scholars should glorify the black man in America and awaken him to his heroic past. The attack on Styron's *Nat Turner,* together with the attack on Ralph Ellison's *Invisible Man* a few years ago as "a vicious distortion of Negro life" depicting Negroes as "Uncle Toms, pimps, sex perverts, guilt-ridden traitors," could easily have been written by Mike Gold.[7] In resisting this type of criticism, always so tempting to radicals, *Partisan Review* performed a service that has to be performed again, it would seem, in every generation. It kept alive a

---

[6] Maxwell Geismar: "Year of Revelations," *The Minority of One,* December 1967, pp. 13, 14–15. In the same article Geismar praises my article, "The Cultural Cold War." I am grateful for the praise but regret to see the article used to support a cultural point of view I find repugnant. For Gold's attack on Dreiser see Aaron: *Writers on the Left,* pp. 276–8.

[7] John O. Killens, quoted in Cruse: *The Crisis of the Negro Intellectual,* p. 235.

literary tradition repeatedly threatened with extinction, and broadened and deepened the understanding of that tradition as well.

The magazine did not, however, achieve a successful fusion of politics and culture. This failure was inevitable, given the absence of a mass base for radicalism in the United States. The only thing even approaching a mass radical movement in the thirties was the Communist party, which ultimately had to be rejected for obvious reasons. In the absence of a mass movement, literary radicals could hope for social change only by postulating the intellectuals themselves as a kind of revolutionary "International."[8] This position, however, merely reinforced the intellectuals' isolation. Worse, it contributed to the retreat from politics which in the forties led most of the radicals of the 1930's to renounce radicalism altogether. By the mid-forties, the editors of *Partisan Review,* horrified by Stalinism in Russia and weary of inconclusive struggles at home, were taking the position that politics at best offered "partial answers" to questions.[9] In the context of generally diminished political expectations, this view melted almost indistinguishably into the retreat from ideology and the emerging postwar "realism." A 1948 symposium on "The State of American Writing" showed what was happening: the defense of "high culture" had come to be identified almost exclusively with anti-Stalinism, while the search for "alternatives to naturalism," as Leslie Fiedler put it in one of the contributions to this discussion, took on the quality of a search for alternatives to politics in general.[1] In 1950 *PR* devoted several issues to "Religion and the Intellectuals"—an ominous sign of the

---

[8] Gilbert: *Writers and Partisans,* p. 192.
[9] Ibid., p. 270 *n.*
[1] *Partisan Review,* August 1948, p. 870.

times, marking a further stage in the retreat from politics, since the kind of religious commitment under consideration tended to focus not on social issues but on what Dwight Macdonald called the "small questions"—"What is a good life? . . . How can I live lovingly, truthfully, pleasurably?"[2] By 1952 the accommodation of literary intellectuals was complete. Noting that American intellectuals had "ceased to think of themselves as rebels and exiles," *Partisan Review* announced a symposium on "Our Country and Our Culture." The "reconciliation" of the intellectuals, according to Rahv, reflected not merely the collapse of "Utopian illusions and heady expectations" of the thirties but American culture's coming of age. "The passage of time has considerably blunted the edge of the old Jamesian complaint as to the barrenness of the native scene."[3] Most of the contributors to "Our Country and Our Culture" agreed with this optimistic assessment of American culture, even though they could give no convincing reasons for doing so; indeed they all deplored "mass culture." Rahv himself admitted, moreover, that "the rout of the left-wing movement has depoliticized literature" and given rise to "a kind of detachment from principle and fragmentation of the literary life." Yet the illusion persisted that in rejecting "extreme ideas," intellectuals had become "more open to the persuasions of actuality."[4] Norman Mailer found the entire symposium "shocking"; and it is hard to avoid his judgment that the fashionable sneers at economics and the concern with "the human dilemma," reversing without correcting the distorted perspectives of the thirties, indicated a pervasive belief that "society is too difficult to understand and history impossible

---

[2] Ibid., May–June 1950, p. 479.
[3] Ibid., May–June 1952, pp. 284, 304–5.
[4] Ibid., pp. 309, 304.

to predict"—indicated, that is, a wholesale defection of intellectuals from social criticism.[5]

This capitulation not only contributed to the cold war, it obscured the degree to which American culture, far from having reached maturity, remained essentially what it had been in the thirties, when the editors of *Partisan Review* launched their campaign for an international culture. In spite of their efforts, American culture remained primitive and provincial; but instead of reminding their readers of this fact, the editors now allowed themselves to be diverted into a polemic against "middlebrow" culture. Emphasis on this issue made it difficult to see the more important point that "we are still," as Steven Marcus wrote in *PR* in 1958, "a provincial and decentralized society, a society without a center of cultural intelligence and sanity." Marcus himself neglected to point out that not only the second-rate but even the highest products of such a culture are necessarily "eccentric and provincial."[6] Nor did anyone writing for *Partisan Review* point out that this cultural failure both reflects and contributes to the failure of radical politics. Not only literature and literary criticism but critical thought in general suffers from the spiritual and philosophical chaos of American life. The correction of this condition ought to be the work of an intellectual class committed not only to the most rigorous standards of critical scholarship but to a thoroughgoing transformation of American institutions. But the emergence of a class committed to these objectives depends, among other things, on the expectation that social change is a real alternative and not merely a theoretical possibility. It depends, in other words, on the existence of mass move-

[5] Ibid., pp. 299–300.
[6] Steven Marcus: "Three Obsessed Critics," in William Phillips and Philip Rahv, eds.: *The Partisan Review Anthology* (New York: Holt, Rinehart, and Winston; 1962), p. 477.

ments for change, based not on alienated intellectuals but on the needs of large numbers of people in their working lives. In the fifties, however, Dwight Macdonald expressed an undeniable truth when he observed that "in terms of mass action, . . . our problems appear to be insoluble."[7]

The hopes of the thirties having expired, the stage was set for the revival of the cultural "International" in a new and remarkably unattractive form: the Congress for Cultural Freedom.

---

[7] *Partisan Review,* May–June 1950, p. 479.

THE CULTURAL COLD WAR: A SHORT HISTORY OF THE CONGRESS FOR CULTURAL FREEDOM

THE CONGRESS FOR CULTURAL FREEDOM WAS FOUNDED in 1950. Even to outward appearances, it had a quasi-official character. Of the two men most active in promoting the organization, one, Michael Josselson, was a former officer in the Office of Strategic Services, while the other, Melvin J. Lasky, had earlier served in the American Information Service and as editor of *Der Monat,* a magazine sponsored by the United States High Commission in Germany. The decision to hold the first meeting of the congress in West Berlin, an outpost of Western power in Communist East Europe and one of the principal foci and symbols of the cold war, fitted very well the official American policy of making Berlin a showcase of "freedom." The United Press reported in advance that "the five-day meeting will challenge the alleged freedoms of Soviet-dominated Eastern Europe and attempt to unmask the Soviet Union's and Soviet-sponsored 'peace' demonstrations as purely political maneuvers."[1] H. R. Trevor-Roper, one of the British delegates, noted that "a political tone was set and maintained throughout the congress." Nobody would have objected to a political demonstration, he observed, if it had been avowed as such. The question was whether "it would have obtained all its sponsors or all its delegates if it had been correctly advertised."[2]

[1] *The New York Times,* June 26, 1950.
[2] *Manchester Guardian Weekly,* July 20, 1950.

The sponsors of the meeting included such eminent fig-
ures as Eleanor Roosevelt, Upton Sinclair, the philosophers
G. A. Borgese and A. J. Ayer, Walter Reuther, the French
writer Suzanne Labin, and Dr. Hans Thirring, a Viennese
atomic scientist. Delegates attended from twenty-one countries, but the most conspicuous among them were militant
anticommunists (some of them also ex-Communists) from
the European continent and from the United States: Arthur
Koestler, Franz Borkenau of Austria, Melvin J. Lasky, Sidney Hook, James Burnham, James T. Farrell, Arthur
Schlesinger, Jr. A number of themes quickly emerged from
their speeches which would become polemical staples in the
following decade. One was the end of ideology, the assertion that conventional political distinctions had become irrelevant in the face of the need for a united front against
Bolshevism. Koestler announced that "the words 'socialism'
and 'capitalism,' 'left' and 'right' have today become virtually empty of meaning."[3] Hook looked forward "to the era
when references to 'right,' 'left,' and 'center' will vanish from
common usage as meaningless."[4] Borkenau made the same
point and went on to explain the deeper sense in which
ideology could be said to have died.[5] "We are living," he

[3] Ibid.

[4] *The New York Times*, June 27, 1950.

[5] References to Borkenau in the following discussion are based on
a translation of his prepared address by G. L. Arnold which appeared
in *The Nineteenth Century*, November 1950, pp. 300–5. Borkenau
also delivered an extemporaneous speech which was described by
Trevor-Roper in the *Manchester Guardian Weekly*, July 20, 1950, as
follows: "Pouring out his German sentences with hysterical speed
and gestures, he screamed that he was a convert from communism
and proud of it; that past guilt must be atoned for; that the ex-Communists alone understood communism and the means of resisting it;
that communism could only mean perpetual war and civil war; and
that it must be destroyed at once by uncompromising frontal attack.
And yet, terrible though it was, this fanatical speech was less

said, in "the last phase of an ebbing revolutionary epoch" in which "the absurdity of the belief in perfect and logical social constructions" had been exposed for all to see. For more than a century utopian "extremes"—visions of total freedom competing with visions of total security—had "increasingly turned the history of the occident into a tragic bedlam." But having observed at first hand the devastating effects of utopianism, particularly in Russia, reasonable men had at last learned the importance of a more modest and pragmatic view of politics.

Pragmatism, however, did not mean that a moral man could remain neutral in the struggle of competing ideologies. Robert Montgomery, the American film actor, declared that "no artist who has the right to bear that title can be neutral in the battles of our time. . . . Today we must stand up and be counted."[6] "In varying phraseology and in different languages but concentrating on one basic point, delegates . . . admonished listeners," according to the correspondent of *The New York Times*, ". . . that the time is at hand for a decision as between the East and West." "Man stands at a crossroads," Koestler said, "which only leaves the choice of this way or that." At such moments, "the difference between the very clever and the simple in mind narrows almost to the vanishing point"; and only the "pro-

---

frightening than the hysterical German applause which greeted it. It was different from any other applause at that congress. It was an echo of Hitler's Nuremberg."

Arnold charged that Trevor-Roper's account created "misleading impressions." "No one would have guessed from Mr. Trevor-Roper's report . . . that one of the calmest and weightiest contributions was made by Dr. Borkenau—in writing." (*The Nineteenth Century*, November 1950, p. 295.) In dealing with this latter speech, therefore, we are dealing with what passed for calm and weighty political analysis in 1950.

[6] *The New York Times*, June 28, 1950.

fessional disease" of the intellectual, his fascination with
logical subtleties and his "estrangement from reality," kept
him from seeing the need to choose between slavery and
freedom.[7]

The attack on liberal intellectualism, and on liberalism in
general, ran through a number of speeches. Borkenau
argued that totalitarianism grew dialectically out of liberalism. "The liberal utopia of absolute individual freedom
found its counterpart in the socialist utopia of complete
individual security." With liberalism in decline, intellectuals
looking for "a ready-made doctrine of salvation and a pre-
fabricated paradise" turned in the twenties and thirties to
communism and "permitted themselves to be led by the
nose through Russia without noticing anything of the reality." During the Second World War—which Borkenau
called "a second edition of the Popular Front"—even experienced politicians allowed themselves to be deceived by
Stalin's professions of good faith. "Thus in the course of a
quarter century communism ran a course which brought it
in contact with every stratum of society, from extreme revolutionaries to ultra-conservatives." But this very pervasive-
ness, by another turn of Borkenau's dialectic, meant that
"the entire body of occidental society has received an increasingly strong protective inoculation against communism. Every new wave of Communist expansion led to a
deepening of the anti-Communist current: from the ineffective opposition of small groups to the rise of an intellectual
countercurrent, and finally to the struggle in the arena of
world politics."

The attack on liberalism, together with the curious argument that exposure to communism was the only effective
form of "inoculation" against it, points to another feature

[7] Ibid., June 26, 1950.

of the anticommunist mentality as revealed at Berlin: a strong undercurrent of ex-communism, which led Trevor-Roper to describe the whole conference as "an alliance between . . . the ex-communists among the delegates . . . and the German nationalists in the audience."[8] Borkenau, Koestler, Burnham, and Hook, among others, had been communists during the thirties, and it requires no special powers of discernment to see that their attack on communism in the fifties expressed itself in formulations that were themselves derived from the cruder sort of Marxist cant. Borkenau's defense of "freedom," for instance, rested not on a concern for institutional safeguards of free thought, let alone for the independence of critical thought from national power, but rather on an assertion of man's capacity to transcend the "narrow materialism" posited, according to Borkenau, by liberalism and socialism alike. The defense of freedom merged imperceptibly with the dogmatic attack on historical materialism which, in another context, has done so much to impede historical and sociological scholarship in the period of the cold war. It is significant that Borkenau still regarded Leninism as a "great achievement," not, however, because Lenin had contributed to the materialist interpretation of society but because Lenin rejected Marx's "fatalism" and converted socialism "into the free act of a determined, ruthless and opportunist elite." Elitism was one of the things that attracted intellectuals to Leninism in the first place (more than to orthodox Marxism); and even after they had dissociated themselves from its materialist content, they clung to the congenial view of intellectuals as the vanguard of history and to the crude and simplified dialectic (of which Borkenau's speech is an excellent example, and James Burnham's *The Managerial Revolu-*

---

[8] *Manchester Guardian Weekly,* July 20, 1950.

tion another) which passed for Marxism in left-wing circles of the thirties.

These things not only demonstrate the amazing persistence and tenacity of the Bolshevik habit of mind even among those who now rejected whatever was radical and liberating in Bolshevism, they also suggest the way in which a certain type of anticommunist intellectual continued to speak from a point of view "alienated" from bourgeois liberalism. Anticommunism, for such men as Koestler and Borkenau, represented a new stage in their running polemic against bourgeois sentimentality and weakness, bourgeois "utopianism." and bourgeois materialism. That explains their eagerness to connect Bolshevism with liberalism—to show that the two ideologies sprang from a common root and that it was the softness and sentimentality of bourgeois liberals which had paradoxically allowed communism (liberalism's deadly enemy, one might have supposed) to pervade Western society in the thirties and early forties. In attributing "twenty years of treason" to an alliance between liberals and communists, the anticommunist intellectuals put forth their own version of the right-wing ideology that was gaining adherents, in a popular and still cruder form, in all the countries of the West, particularly in Germany and the United States. In the fifties, this high-level McCarthyism sometimes served as a defense of McCarthyism proper. More often it was associated with official efforts to pre-empt a modified McCarthyism while denouncing McCarthy as a demagogue. In both capacities it contributed measurably to the cold war.

At still another point on its multifaceted surface, the ideology of the anticommunist Left tended to merge with fascism, which has served as yet another vehicle for the intellectual's attack on bourgeois materialism. Borkenau, for instance—in so many ways the embodiment of a central

European, quasi-totalitarian sensibility—denounced totalitarianism at length without referring, except in passing and in the most general terms, to its most horrifying manifestation, the Nazi regime in Germany. In the United States anticommunism found a more congenial basis in political pragmatism, which, however, shared with European neofascism the capacity to furnish a perspective—a quite different perspective—from which to belabor "utopianism." And whereas the elitism of European intellectuals expressed itself in a cult of charismatic leadership, the American variety based its distrust of the masses precisely on their susceptibility to extreme political solutions; that is, to the same utopianism which the Europeans attacked as a vice of deluded intellectuals. Thus a neat twist of logic permitted those who opposed McCarthyism to argue that McCarthyism was itself a form of populism. This condemned it sufficiently in the eyes of a generation that tended to confuse intellectual values with the interests of the intellectuals as a class, just as they confused freedom with the national interests of the United States.

[II]

The Berlin meetings, meanwhile, broke up in a spirit of rancor which must have alarmed those who had hoped for a united front against Bolshevism. A resolution excluding totalitarian sympathizers "from the Republic of the Spirit" was withdrawn, "Professor Hook and Mr. Burnham," according to Trevor-Roper, "protesting to the end." The opposition came largely from the English and Scandinavian delegates—a revealing fact for two reasons. In the first place it showed how closely the division of opinion among intellectuals, who supposedly take a more detached view of things than governments do, coincided with the distribution of power in the world. In 1950, the United States had already emerged as the leader of an anticommunist coalition on the European continent, and Great Britain had fallen into her role of a reluctant and not very influential member of a partnership which increasingly tended to revolve around the West Germans. The discussions at Berlin—even the choice of the meeting place—accurately reflected these political facts.

In the second place, the reluctance of the British delegates to join a rhetorical crusade against communism, in this first of the postwar struggles for cultural freedom, seems to have suggested to the officers of the Congress for Cultural Freedom that British intellectuals needed to be approached more energetically than before, if they were not to lapse completely into the heresy of neutralism. Koestler, at Berlin, had already berated England as parochial and isolationist for refusing to see the simplicity of the choice confronting the twentieth-century intellectual.[9] The founding of *Encounter* magazine in 1953, with Irving Kristol, Stephen Spender, and later Lasky at its head, was the official answer to the "anti-Americanism," as it was now called, which disfigured the English cultural scene. The editors of *Encounter* addressed themselves with zeal to its destruction.

The new magazine lost no time in establishing its point of view and its characteristic tone of ultra-sophistication. The

---

[9] In *The God That Failed* (Richard Crossman, ed. [New York: Bantam Books; 1952], pp. 1–2), Koestler told Richard Crossman: "Either you can't or you won't understand. It's the same with all you comfortable, insular, Anglo-Saxon anti-Communists. You hate our Cassandra cries and resent us as allies—but when all is said, we ex-Communists are the only people on your side who know what it's all about."

very first issue contained a spirited polemic on the Rosenberg case by Leslie Fiedler, whose uncanny instinct for cultural fashions, combined with a gift for racy language ("Come Back to the Raft Ag'in, Huck Honey"), made him a suitable spokesman for cultural freedom in the fifties. Fiedler had already, in "Hiss, Chambers, and the Age of Innocence," exhorted intellectuals to accept their common guilt in the crimes of Alger Hiss.[1] With an equal disregard for the disputed facts of the case, he now went on to berate sentimentalists who still believed the Rosenbergs to be innocent. "As far as I am concerned the legal guilt of the Rosenbergs was clearly established at their trial."[2] From the fact of their guilt, Fiedler spun an intricate web of theory intended to show, once again, what a pervasive and deplorable influence Stalinism had exercised, for twenty years, over the life of the mind in America. Years later it turned out that the central document which had been used to convict the Rosenbergs was a crude forgery. The "atomic secrets" which the Rosenbergs allegedly handed over to the Soviet Union proved to be a "caricature" of the bomb, according to an eminent atomic scientist, "too incomplete, ambiguous, and even incorrect to be of any service or value to the Russians."[3]

---

[1] *Commentary*, August 1951, pp. 109–19; reprinted in Leslie Fiedler: *An End to Innocence* (Boston: Beacon Press; 1955), pp. 3–24. See also Fiedler's "McCarthy" (*Encounter*, August 1954, pp. 10–21), in which he pooh-poohed "the loud fears of the intellectuals" and made McCarthyism the occasion for another attack on the "outlived illusions of the Left."

[2] "A Postscript to the Rosenburg Case," *Encounter*, October 1953, p. 13; *An End to Innocence*, p. 27.

[3] Philip Morison, quoted in *The New York Times*, August 28, 1966. Dr. Henry Linschitz, who helped to assemble the atomic bomb at Los Alamos, said: "It is astonishing . . . that the layman still clings to the misconception that there is a 'secret' or key

"To believe that two innocents had been falsely condemned," Fiedler argued, ". . . one would have to believe the judges and public officials of the United States to be not merely the Fascists the Rosenbergs called them, but monsters, insensate beasts."[4] Whereas in fact, the implication seemed to be, they were dedicated humanitarians. Just so; and in order to believe that the CIA had infiltrated (for example) the National Student Association, one would have to believe—heaven forbid!—that the CIA was a corrupter of youth. The absurdity of such a thing is self-evident; the case collapses of its own weight.

For a group of intellectuals who prided themselves on their realism, skepticism, and detachment (qualities they regularly displayed in cogent analyses of the deplorable state of affairs in Soviet Russia), the editors of *Encounter* and their contributors showed an unshakable faith in the good intentions of the American government. It was inconceivable to them that American officials were not somehow immune to the temptations of great power. The defense of "cultural freedom" was wholly entwined, in their minds, with the defense of the "free world" against communism. Criticism of the men who presided over the free world— even mild criticism—tended automatically to exclude itself from their minds as a subject for serious discussion. These men might make occasional mistakes; but there could be no question of their devotion to freedom.

"*Encounter*," wrote Denis Brogan (a frequent contributor) in 1963, "has been the organ of protest against the

---

'formula' for the construction of an atomic bomb. This notion was even more obsessively held at the time of the Rosenburg-Sobell trial." (Ibid.)

[4] *Encounter*, October 1953, pp. 20–1; *An End to Innocence*, pp. 44–5.

trahison des clercs."[5] Julian Benda's point, in the book from which Brogan took this phrase, was that intellectuals should serve truth, not power. *Encounter*'s claim to be the defender of intellectual values in a world dominated by ideology rested, therefore, on its vigorous criticism of all influences tending to undermine critical thought, whether they emanated from the Soviet Union or from the United States. This is indeed the claim that the editors and friends of *Encounter* have made. As we shall see, the cold-war liberals have not hesitated to criticize American popular culture or popular politics, but the question is whether they have criticized the American government or any other aspect of the officially sanctioned order. And the fact is that *Encounter,* like other journals sponsored by the Congress for Cultural Freedom (except perhaps for *Censorship,* which recently expired), consistently approved the broad lines and even the details of American policy, until the war in Vietnam shattered the cold-war coalition and introduced a new phase of American politics. Writers in *Encounter* denounced the Soviet intervention in Hungary without drawing the same conclusions about the Bay of Pigs.[6] They

[5] Quoted in Conor Cruise O'Brien: *Writers and Politics* (New York: Pantheon Books; 1966), p. 169.

[6] Melvin J. Lasky has pointed out: "In July, 1961, *Encounter* published a 15,000-word analysis by Theodore Draper criticizing the 'perfect failure' of U.S. policy toward Cuba; in the next number Anthony Hartley explained, from a British writer's viewpoint, why the 'disastrous adventure' was shocking, illegal and wrong. In July, 1964, *Encounter* published a 9,000-word article by Herbert L. Matthews, entitled 'Dissent over Cuba,' protesting the perils of nonconformity in the U.S. and the dangers of dissent which he himself and other friends of Castro's Cuba had experienced." (*The Nation,* October 2, 1967, p. 309.)

The Draper article, however, criticized American policy within

had little if anything to say about the American coup in Guatemala, the CIA's intervention in Iran, its role in the creation of Diem, or the American support of Trujillo; but they regarded communist "colonialism" with horror. The plight of the communist satellites wrung their hearts; that of South Korea and South Vietnam left them unmoved. They denounced racism in the Soviet Union while ignoring it in South Africa and the United States until it was no longer possible to ignore it, at which time (1952) *Encounter* published an overly optimistic issue on the "Negro Crisis," the general tone of which was quite consistent with the optimism then being purveyed by the Kennedy administration.

In 1958, Dwight Macdonald submitted an article to *Encounter*—"America! America!"—in which he wondered whether the intellectuals' rush to rediscover their native land (one of the obsessive concerns of the fifties, at almost every level of cultural life) had not produced a somewhat uncritical acquiescence in the American *imperium*. The editors told Macdonald to publish his article elsewhere; in the correspondence that followed, according to Macdonald,

---

the framework of cold-war assumptions. Anthony Hartley condemned intervention on the curious ground that subversion of another country violated international law unless justified by internal disorder or "an almost unanimous opinion abroad of the undesirable character of a regime." He specifically denied any parallel between Cuba and Hungary. "American troops were not used, and the operations failed because of it. Can we imagine a genuinely imperialistic regime behaving like this?" (*Encounter*, August 1961, pp. 60, 62) As for the Matthews article, the editors printed it with an apologetic introduction to the effect that although Matthews's views on Cuba had "been frequently criticized in *Encounter*, especially in Theodore Draper's articles," his "account of his opinions and tribulations, especially in the American context, seems to us a document interesting and important enough to publish and to discuss." (Ibid., July 1964, p. 82)

"the note sounded more than once . . . that publication of my article might embarrass the congress in its relations with the American foundations which support it."[7] When the incident became public, Nicholas Nabokov, secretary-general of the congress, pointed in triumph to the fact that Macdonald's article had eventually appeared in *Tempo Presente,* an Italian periodical sponsored by the congress. That proved, he said, that the Paris headquarters of the congress did not dictate editorial policy to the magazines it supported. But the question was not whether the Paris office dictated to the editors what they could publish and what they could not; the question was whether the editors did not take it upon themselves to avoid displeasing the sponsors, whoever they were, standing behind the Congress for Cultural Freedom. The reference to "American foundations," in their correspondence with Macdonald, seemed to suggest that the editors exercised a degree of self-censorship, partly conscious and partly unconscious, that made any other form of censorship unnecessary. It was possible that they had so completely assimilated the official point of view that they were no longer aware of the way in which their writings had come to serve as rationalizations of American world power.

[III]

The Congress for Cultural Freedom, growing directly out of the postwar power struggle in Europe, centered most of its attention on Europe, as did American foreign policy in the fifties, but it did not neglect the rest of the world. In

[7] *Universities and Left Review,* Spring 1959, p. 60.

1951 it sponsored a large conference in India, attended by such luminaries as Denis de Rougemont, W. H. Auden, Stephen Spender, Ignazio Silone, Louis Fischer, Norman Thomas, and, of course, James Burnham, without whom, in those early days, no gathering of the congress was complete. The *Times*'s correspondent understated the case when he wrote that "many of the delegates are said to be former Communists, who have become critics." He noted further: "The meeting has been described as an answer to the 'World Peace Conference' supported by the Soviet Union."[8] The Berlin conference of the year before, it will be recalled, was also conceived as a response to Soviet "peace propaganda." Its immediate stimulus was a series of peace congresses in East Germany.

The delegates meeting in India hoped to bring home to the nonaligned nations the immorality of neutralism. Anne O'Hare McCormick wrote in one of her dispatches: "There is no middle ground in the world conflict"; that was the message which the congress hoped to impress on the Indians.[9] When transferred to a non-Western setting, however, the reiteration of this theme, which had gone down so well with the Berliners, led to an "unexpected undertone of dissatisfaction," according to the *Times*.[1] When Denis de Rougemont "compared the present Indian neutrality with that of the lamb that is neutral between the wolf and the shepherd," one of the Indian delegates drew from the fable a moral quite different from the one intended. He pointed out that the shepherd, having saved the lamb from the wolf, "shears the lamb and possibly eats it."[2] Many Indians boycotted the congress because it had been "branded widely as

[8] *The New York Times,* February 26, 1951.
[9] Ibid., February 5, 1951.
[1] Ibid., March 29, 1951.
[2] Ibid.

a U.S. propaganda device."[3] The Indian government took pains to withhold its official sanction from the meeting, insisting that it be moved from New Delhi, the capital and original site of the conference, to Bombay.

It seemed at times that the Indians did not want to be free. Robert Trumbull, a correspondent of the *Times*, tried to reassure his readers about their "peculiar" point of view. The Indian speakers weren't really neutralists, they were only "manifesting the common Indian oratorial tendency to stray from the real point of the issue in hand."[4] A dispassionate observer might have concluded that they understood the point all too well. The congress, having suffered a rebuff, made no more direct attacks on neutralism in the Third World. In 1958 it held a conference on the problems of developing nations, but the tone of this meeting differed noticeably from the one in Bombay.[5] The conference, meeting on the isle of Rhodes, produced no notable results. Probably it was not expected to have any. Already the global struggle for cultural freedom seemed to have entered a new phase, in which the crudely propagandist flavor of the Berlin and Bombay meetings had given way to a new worldliness, a new sophistication—about neutralism, for example—that heralded the coming of the New Frontier. A new official style was emerging, faithfully reflected in the

---

[3] Ibid., March 30, 1951.

[4] Ibid., March 31, 1951.

[5] It was on the second of these occasions that Richard Rovere described the Congress for Cultural Freedom as "a worthy organization, anti-Communist and generally libertarian in outlook and associated with no government." He went on to say: "The Congress for Cultural Freedom is more interested in philosophers than in kings, and in the Western nations it is easy to tell one class from the other; indeed, it is almost impossible to confuse the two. . . . By and large, the rule in the West is that intellectuals and politicians stay out of each other's way." (*The New Yorker*, November 8, 1958, pp. 171–2.)

Congress for Cultural Freedom—urbane, cool and bureau-cratic. The old slogans had become passé, even as the old policies continued. The union of intellect and power decep-tively presented itself as an apparent liberalization of official attitudes, an apparent relaxation of American anticom-munism. McCarthyism was dead and civilized conversation in great demand. The Congress for Cultural Freedom no longer proselytized; to everyone's delight, it spon-sored conversation—bounded, of course, by the limits of rational discourse, the agreed-upon end of ideology, but with no other visible strings attached. The congress flew people to Rhodes and encouraged them to participate in a highly civilized, nonideological discussion of economic development—a gratifying experience for everybody con-cerned, all the more so since it made so few demands on the participants. Expansive and tolerant, the congress asked only that intellectuals avail themselves of the increasing op-portunities for travel and enlightenment that the defense of freedom made possible.

[IV]

Shortly after the founding of the Congress for Cultural Freedom, its more active members set up subsidiaries in various countries. The American Committee for Cultural Freedom was founded in 1951 by Burnham, Farrell, Schlesinger, Hook, and others, to hold annual forums on such topics as "The Ex-Communist: His Role in a Democ-racy" or "Anti-Americanism in Europe"; to "counteract the influence of mendacious Communist propaganda" (for in-stance, "the Communist assertion that the Rosenbergs were victimized innocents"); to defend academic freedom; and in general "to resist the lengthening shadow of thought-control."[6] The committee had a limited though illustrious membership, never exceeding six hundred, and it subsisted on grants from the congress and on public contributions. It repeatedly made public appeals for money, even announcing, in 1957, that it was going out of business for lack of funds.[7] It survived; but ever since that time it has been semi-moribund, for reasons that will become clearer in a moment.

Sidney Hook was the first chairman of the ACCF. He was succeeded in 1952 by George S. Counts of Teachers College, Columbia, who was followed in 1954 by Robert Gorham Davis of Smith. James T. Farrell, who took Davis's place in the same year, resigned in 1956 after a quarrel with other members of the committee. Traveling in the Third World, he had come to the conclusion that foreign aid was a waste of money and that the Indians, for instance, believed that their best policy was "to flirt with Communists, insult us and perhaps get more money out of us." In a letter written from Turkey and published in *The Chicago Tribune,* Farrell insisted that American aid should be given only on condition that the recipients join the United States in "a truly honest partnership in freedom"; otherwise Americans "should retire to our own shores" and "go it alone."[8]

Diana Trilling, chairman of the administrative committee of the American Committee for Cultural Freedom, attacked Farrell's letter on the ground that it "sullied his long record as a champion of understanding among the free peoples of the world." Anyone expressing such opinions, she said, was "not suited" for the chairmanship of the ACCF. Farrell, in resigning, said that "his travels had convinced

---

[6] *The American Committee for Cultural Freedom,* pamphlet, n.d. [New York, 1953], p. 2.

[7] *The New York Times,* March 4, 1957.

[8] Quoted in ibid., August 29, 1956.

him that he and other members had been 'wrong' in earlier
struggles against Paris office policies."[9] His statement, incidentally, suggests that the Paris office sometimes tried to
enforce its own views on subsidiary organizations, in spite
of its disclaimers. It also shows—what should already be
apparent—that the congress in its early period took a very
hard line on neutralism.

Farrell's resignation, along with other events, signaled the
breakdown of the coalition on which the American committee was based, a coalition of moderate liberals and reactionaries (both groups including a large number of
ex-communists) held together by their mutual obsession
with the communist conspiracy. James Burnham had already
resigned in 1954. Earlier Burnham had resigned as a member
of the advisory board of *Partisan Review* (which since 1959
has been sponsored by the American Committee for
Cultural Freedom) in a dispute with the editors over Mc-
Carthyism. Burnham approved of McCarthy's actions and
held that McCarthyism was a "diversionary" issue created
by communists. William Phillips and Philip Rahv, adopting
a favorite slogan of the cold war to their own purposes, announced, however, that there was no room on *Partisan Review* for "neutralism" about McCarthy.[1]

Originally, the ACCF took quite literally the assertion,
advanced by Koestler and others at Berlin, that the communist issue overrode conventional distinctions between
Left and Right. Right-wingers like Burnham, Farrell, Ralph
De Toledano, John Chamberlain, John Dos Passos, and
even Whittaker Chambers consorted with Schlesinger,
Hook, Irving Kristol, Daniel Bell, and other liberals. In the

[9] Ibid.
[1] *Partisan Review,* November–December 1953, pp. 716–17; *The
New York Times,* November 15, 1953.

early fifties, this uneasy alliance worked because the liberals generally took positions that conceded a good deal of ground to the Right, if they were not indistinguishable from those of the Right. But the end of the Korean War and the censure of McCarthy in 1954 created a slightly less oppressive air in which the right-wing rhetoric of the early fifties seemed increasingly inappropriate to political realities. Now that McCarthy was dead as a political force, the liberals courageously attacked him, thereby driving the Right out of the Committee for Cultural Freedom. The collapse of the anticommunist coalition coincided in turn with the committee's financial crisis of 1957 and with the beginning of its long period of inactivity.

These three developments presumably were related. The ACCF and its parent, the Congress for Cultural Freedom, took shape in a period of the cold war when official anticommunism had not clearly distinguished itself, rhetorically, from the anticommunism of the Right. In a later period official liberalism, having taken over essential features of the rightist world view, belatedly dissociated itself from the cruder and blatantly reactionary type of anticommunism, and now pursued the same anticommunist policies in the name of anti-imperialism and progressive change. Once again, the Kennedy administration contributed decisively to the change of style, placing more emphasis on counterinsurgency than on military alliances, advocating an Alliance for Progress, de-emphasizing military aid in favor of development, refraining from attacks on neutralism, and presenting itself as the champion of democratic revolution in the undeveloped world.

The practical result of the change was a partial *détente* with communism in Europe and a decidedly more aggressive policy in the rest of the world (made possible by that *détente*), of which the most notable products were the Bay of Pigs, the Dominican intervention, and the war in Vietnam. The European *détente* made the anticommunist rhetoric of the fifties obsolete, although it of course did not make anticommunism obsolete. The particular brand of anticommunism that flourished in the fifties grew out of the postwar power struggles in Europe and out of traumas of twentieth-century history—fascism, Stalinism, the crisis of liberal democracy—all of which had concerned Europe, not Asia. The prototype of the anticommunist intellectual in the fifties was the disillusioned ex-communist, obsessed by the corruption of Western politics and culture by the pervasive influence of Stalinism and driven by a need to exercise the evil and expatiate his own past. The anticommunism of the sixties on the other hand, focused on the Third World and demanded another kind of rhetoric.

[V]

The ACCF, then, represented a coalition of liberals and reactionaries who shared a conspiratorial view of communism and who agreed, moreover, that the communist conspiracy had spread through practically every level of American society. (It is the adherence of liberals to these dogmas that shows how much they had conceded to the right-wing view of history.) Sidney Hook's "Heresy, Yes—Conspiracy, No!" published in *The New York Times Magazine* in 1950–51 and distributed as a pamphlet by the ACCF, set forth the orthodox position and tried to distinguish it (not very successfully) from that of the Right, as well as from "ritualistic liberalism." Heresy—the open expression of dissenting opinions—had to be distinguished, according to Hook, from secret movements seeking to attain their ends "not by normal political or educational processes but by playing outside the rules of the game." This distinction did not lead Hook to conclude that communism, insofar as it was a heresy as opposed to a conspiracy, was entitled to constitutional protection. On the contrary, he argued that communism was a conspiracy by its very nature—a point he sought to establish by quotations from Lenin and Stalin which purportedly revealed a grand design for world conquest. Since they were members of an international conspiracy—servants of a foreign power—communists could not expect to enjoy the same liberties enjoyed by other Americans.

The committee's official position on academic freedom started from the same premise. "A member of the Communist Party has transgressed the canons of academic responsibility, has engaged his intellect to servility, and is therefore professionally disqualified from performing his functions as scholar and teacher." The committee on academic freedom (Counts, Hook, Arthur O. Lovejoy, Paul R. Hays) characteristically went on to argue that the matter of communists should be left "in the hands of the colleges, and their faculties." "There is no justification for a Congressional committee to concern itself with the question."[2] Academic freedom meant self-determination for the academic community. The full implications of this position will be explored in due time.

"Liberalism in the twentieth century," Sidney Hook declared in the spirit of the Berlin manifesto, "must toughen its fibre, for it is engaged in a fight on many different fronts."[3] A sentimental and unrealistic tradition of uncriti-

---

[2] *The New York Times,* July 19, 1953.
[3] "Heresy, Yes—Conspiracy, No!" (New York: American Committee for Cultural Freedom, n.d.). All the following references are to this pamphlet, pp. 14, 16, 17.

cal tolerance might prove to be a fatal handicap in the struggle with totalitarianism. "Ritualistic liberals," according to Hook, not only failed to distinguish between heresy and conspiracy, they helped to "weaken the moral case of Western democracy against Communist totalitarianism" by deploring witch hunts, giving the unfortunate impression that America was "on the verge of Fascism." He conceded that some demagogues—he tactfully refrained from mentioning them by name—sought to discredit unpopular reforms by unfairly labeling them communist. But the important point was that these activities were not the official policy of "our government," they were the actions of "cultural vigilantes." Ignorant people saw progressive education, for example, or the federal withholding tax, as evidence of communist subversion—an absurdity which suggested to Hook, not the inherent absurdity of the anticommunist ideology, but the absurdity of untutored individuals concerning themselves with matters best left to experts. The student of these events is struck by the way in which ex-communists seem always to have retained the worst of Marx and Lenin and to have discarded the best. The elitism which once glorified intellectuals as a revolutionary avant-garde now glorifies them as experts and social technicians. On the other hand, Marx's insistence that political issues be seen in their social context—his insistence, for example, that questions of taxation are not "technical" but political questions, the solutions to which reflect the type of social organization in which they arise—this social determinism, which makes Marx's ideas potentially so useful as a method of social analysis, has been sloughed off by Hook without a qualm. These reflections lead one to the conclusion, once more, that many intellectuals were more attracted to Marxism in the first place as an elitist and antidemocratic ideology than as a means of analysis which provided not answers but the beginnings of a critical theory of society.

Hook's whole line of argument, with its glorification of experts and its attack on amateurs, reflected one of the dominant values of the modern intellectual—his acute sense of himself as a professional with a vested interest in technical solutions to political problems. Leave education to the educators and taxation to the tax lawyers. Hook's attack on "cultural vigilantism" paralleled the academic interpretation of McCarthyism as a form of populism and a form of anti-intellectualism, except that it did not even go so far as to condemn McCarthyism itself; instead, it focused attention on peripheral issues like progressive education and the withholding tax.

Some liberals, in fact, specifically defended McCarthy. Irving Kristol, in his notorious article in the March 1952 issue of *Commentary,* admitted that McCarthy was a "vulgar demagogue," but added: "There is one thing that the American people know about Senator McCarthy; he, like them, is unequivocally anti-Communist. About the spokesmen for American liberalism, they feel they know no such thing." This article has been cited many times to show how scandalously the anticommunist Left allied itself with the Right. Kristol's article was a scandal, but it was no more a scandal than the apparently more moderate position which condemned unauthorized anticommunism while endorsing the official variety. By defining the issue as "cultural vigilantism," the anticommunist intellectuals lent themselves to the dominant drive of the modern state—not only to eliminate the private use of violence (vigilantism) but, finally, to discredit all criticism which does not come from officially recognized experts. The government had a positive interest in suppressing McCarthy, as the events of the Eisenhower administration showed—not because of any tender solicitude for civil liberties, but because McCarthy's unauthorized anticommunism competed with and disrupted official anticommunist activities like the Voice of America. This point was made again and again during the Army-McCarthy hearings. (The fact that it was the Army that emerged as McCarthy's most powerful antagonist is itself suggestive.) The same point dominated the propaganda of the ACCF. "Government agencies," said Hook, "find their work hampered by the private fevers of cultural vigilantism which have arisen like a rash from the anti-Communist mood." "Constant vigilance," he added, "does not require private citizens to usurp the functions of agencies entrusted with the task of detection and exposure."[4]

In effect—though they would have denied it—the intellectuals of the ACCF defined cultural freedom as whatever best served the interests of the United States government. When James Wechsler was dropped from a television program, the *New Leader* (a magazine which consistently took the same positions as the ACCF) wrote: "This lends substance to the Communist charge that America is hysteria-ridden."[5] Diana Trilling agreed that "the idea that America is a terror-stricken country in the grip of hysteria is a Communist-inspired idea."[6] After McCarthy's attack on the Voice of America, even Hook criticized McCarthy because of "the incalculable harm he is doing to the reputation of the United States abroad."[7] The ACCF officially condemned McCarthy's investigation of the Voice of America. "The net effect, at this crucial moment, has been to frustrate the very possibility of the United States embarking on a program of psychological warfare against world communism."[8] A few

---

[4] "Heresy, Yes—Conspiracy, No!," p. 27.
[5] *New Leader,* August 25, 1952, p. 22.
[6] Ibid., April 28, 1952, p. 16.
[7] *The New York Times,* May 8, 1953.
[8] Ibid., March 9, 1953.

months later, the ACCF announced the appointment of Sol Stein as its executive director. Stein had been a writer and political affairs analyst for the Voice of America. He was succeeded in 1956 by Norman Jacobs, chief political commentator of the Voice of America and head of its Central Radio Features Branch from 1948 to 1955.[9]

While avoiding a principled attack on McCarthyism, the ACCF kept up a running fire on "anti-anticommunism." (It was characteristic of the period that issues so often presented themselves in this sterile form and that positions were formulated not with regard to the substance of a question but with regard to an attitude or "posture" which it was deemed desirable to hold.) In January 1953 the ACCF handed down a directive setting out the grounds on which it was permissible to involve oneself in the Rosenberg case. "[The] pre-eminent fact of the Rosenbergs' guilt must be openly acknowledged before any appeal for clemency can be regarded as having been made in good faith. Those who allow the Communists to make use of their names in such a way as to permit any doubt to arise about the Rosenbergs' guilt are doing a grave disservice to the cause of justice—and of mercy, too."[1]

In 1954 the Emergency Civil Liberties Committee sponsored a conference at Princeton, at which Albert Einstein, along with Corliss Lamont, I. F. Stone, Dirk Struik, and others, urged intellectuals not to cooperate with "witch-hunting" Congressional committees. Sol Stein immediately announced that the ACCF opposed any "exploitation" of academic freedom and civil liberties "by persons who are at this late date still sympathetic to the cause of the Soviet Union." Following its usual practice, the ACCF proceeded

---

[9] Ibid., August 28, 1953; April 10, 1956.
[1] Ibid., January 5, 1953.

to lay down a standard to which any "sincere" criticism of American life, even of McCarthyism, had to conform. "The test of any group's sincerity is whether it is opposed to threats of freedom anywhere in the world and whether it is concerned about the gross suppression of civil liberties and academic freedom behind the Iron Curtain. The Emergency Civil Liberties Committee has not met that test."[2] The validity of criticism, in other words, depended not so much on its substance as on its adherence to a prescribed ritual of dissent.[3]

The ACCF did not stop with this rebuke; it also accused

[2] As late as 1966, one finds Arthur Schlesinger, Jr., still resorting to the same tired old formula, as well as to the catchword, "anti-anticommunism." When Conor Cruise O'Brien accused intellectuals in the West of serving the "power structure" at the same time that they praised Russian writers for resisting the power structure of the Soviet Union (he added that "sympathy with the hard lot of writers in communist countries is sometimes so copiously expressed as to make the lot of these writers actually harder" by alerting bureaucrats to antiparty tendencies they might otherwise have overlooked), Schlesinger, completely avoiding these issues, made the stock response: "How in the year 1966 can anyone, even Mr. O'Brien, write a piece about 'Politics and the Writer' and not mention Sinyavsky and Daniel or their Chinese counterparts?" (*Book Week*, September 11, 1966, p. 6.)

[3] Note the imagery and the ritualistic quality of this passage from an article by Irving Kristol (*Commentary*, March 1952, p. 236): "If a liberal wishes to defend the civil liberties of Communists or of Communist fellow-travelers, he must enter the court of American opinion with clean hands and a clear mind. He must show that he knows the existence of an organized subversive movement such as Communism is a threat to the consensus on which civil society and its liberties are based. He must bluntly acknowledge Communists and fellow-travelers to be what they are, and then, if he so desires, defend the expediency in particular circumstances of allowing them the right to be what they are. He must speak as one of *us*, defending *their* liberties. To the extent he insists that they are on our side, that we can defend our liberties only by uncritically defending theirs, he will be taken as speaking as one of them."

the Emergency Civil Liberties Committee of being "a Communist front with no sincere interest in liberty in the United States or elsewhere."[4] No evidence was adduced to support this statement. The conclusion followed logically, perhaps, from the ACCF's test of "sincerity." The Civil Liberties Committee, in reply, pointed out that even the Attorney-General had not thought to list it as a subversive organization.[5] In this case, the standards of the ACCF were even more rigorous than those of the government itself.

On another occasion, the ACCF tried to plant with the *New York World Telegram and Sun* a story, already circulated by the *New Leader,* that a certain liberal journalist was a "Soviet espionage agent." Sol Stein called the city desk with what he described as a "Junior Alger Hiss" story. The reporter who took the call asked whether the proper place to determine the truth of these charges was not a court of law. Stein replied, in this reporter's words, that "libel suits were a Communist trick to destroy opposition by forcing it to bear the expense of trial." The reporter then asked whether the ACCF was "upholding the right of people to call anyone a Communist without being subject to libel suits." Stein said: "You misunderstand the context of the times. Many reckless charges are being made today. But when the charges are documented, the Committee believes you have the right to say someone is following the Communist line without being brought into court." The reporter asked if Stein had any proof that the journalist in question was a Soviet spy. Stein said no, "but we have mountains of material that show he consistently follows the Soviet line."[6]

When they took positions of which the ACCF disap-

---

[4] *The New York Times,* January 20, 1953.

[5] Ibid.

[6] Confidential memorandum, November 13, 1954, in the files of *The Nation.*

proved the "ritualistic liberals" were communist tools. When they took positions critical of the Soviet Union, the ACCF denied their right to take them. Arthur Miller in 1956 wrote a statement condemning political interference with art in the Soviet Union. The ACCF did not congratulate him; it asked why he had not taken the same position in 1949. The committee also noted that Miller, in any case, had made an unforgivable mistake: he had criticized political interference with art not only in the Soviet Union but in the United States, thereby implying that the two situations were comparable. American incidents, the committee declared, were "episodic violations of the tradition of political and cultural freedom in the United States," whereas "the official government policy" of the USSR was to "impose a 'party line' in all fields of art, culture, and science, and enforcing such a line with sanctions ranging from imprisonment to exile to loss of job." Having dutifully wrapped Miller's knuckles, the ACCF then went on to use his statement by challenging the Soviet government to circulate it in Russia.[7]

[VI]

In 1955 a *New York Times* editorial praised the ACCF for playing a vital role in "the struggle for the loyalty of the world's intellectuals"—in itself a curious way of describing the defense of cultural freedom. The *Times* went on to make the same claim that was so frequently made by the committee itself: "The group's authority to speak for freedom against Communist slavery has been enhanced by its courageous fight against those threatening our own civil liber-

[7] *The New York Times*, February 14, 15, 1956.

ties from the Right."[8] We have already noted that the committee's quarrel with the Right, even though it finally led to the departure of the right-wing members of the committee, was far from "courageous." Even when it found itself confronted with cultural vigilantism in its most obvious forms, the committee stopped short of an unambiguous defense of intellectual freedom. In 1955, for instance, Muhlenberg College canceled a Charlie Chaplin film festival under pressure from a local post of the American Legion. The ACCF protested that "while it is perfectly clear that Chaplin tends to be pro-Soviet and anti-American in his political attitudes, there is no reason why we should not enjoy his excellent movies, which have nothing to do with Communist totalitarianism."[9] This statement left the disturbing implication that if Chaplin's films could be regarded as political, the ban would have been justified. The assertion that art has nothing to do with politics was the poorest possible ground on which to defend cultural freedom.

But whatever the nature of the ACCF's critique of vigilantism, a better test of its "authority to speak for freedom" would have been its willingness to criticize *official* activities in the United States—the real parallel to Soviet repression. (In the Soviet Union, attacks on vigilantism are doubtless not only not proscribed but encouraged. It is attacks on Soviet officials that are not permitted.)

In March 1955 the committee did criticize a Post Office ban on *Pravda* and *Izvestia* as "unreasonable and ineffective in dealing with the Communist conspiracy."[1] A year later the committee deplored the Treasury Department's raid on the office of the *Daily Worker*. "However much we

---

[8] Ibid., March 25, 1955.
[9] Ibid., January 8, 1955.
[1] Ibid., March 4, 1955.

abominate the *Daily Worker,* . . . we must protest even this much interference with the democratic right to publish freely."[2] The ACCF criticized the Agriculture Department's dismissal of Wolf Ladejinsky and the Atomic Energy Commission's persecution of Oppenheimer, in both cases arguing that the victims had established themselves in recent years as impeccably anticommunist.[3] Diana Trilling's article on the Oppenheimer case shows the gingerly fashion in which the ACCF addressed itself to this issue.[4] Although defending Oppenheimer's loyalty, she avoided the question of whether he was being persecuted for his opinions about the H-bomb. Instead she concluded, in the approved style of the ACCF: "Fairness to Dr. Oppenheimer requires that we remind ourselves that our current acute relations with Russia . . . would very likely have never reached their present point of crisis had not so much of the energy of liberalism been directed . . . to persuading the American people that Russia was our great ally."

On one occasion the ACCF attacked the U.S. Information Agency because it canceled an art show in response to charges that four of the artists represented were subversive. Mrs. Trilling insisted that "actions of this kind hold us up to derision abroad." She went on to question the judgment of government officials "who mix politics and art to the detriment of both."[5]

On the other hand, when 360 citizens petitioned the Supreme Court to repeal the 1950 Internal Security Act (which created the Subversive Activities Control Board), James T. Farrell issued a statement for the ACCF calling the petitions "naive," accusing them of a "whitewash" of

[2] Ibid., March 31, 1956.
[3] Ibid., January 4, 1955; April 18, 1954.
[4] *Partisan Review,* November 1954, pp. 604–35.
[5] *The New York Times,* June 9, 1956.

the Communist party, and declaring that if freedom were left in their hands "it would have no future."[6]

The infrequency of complaints against American officials, together with the triviality of the issues that called them forth—as contrasted with the issues against which others protested out of their "naivete"—show that the anticommunist liberals cannot claim to have defended cultural freedom in the United States with the same consistency and vigor with which they defended it in Russia. In the first place, they concerned themselves with the actions of vigilantes at a time when the gravest threat to freedom came from the state. In the second place, even the attack on vigilantism was halfhearted; it was only when McCarthy moved against the Voice of America that the ACCF criticized him at all, and most of the criticism came after he had already been censured by the Senate. Claiming to be the vanguard of the struggle for cultural freedom, the anticommunist intellectuals in reality brought up the rear.

Finally, they based their positions (such positions as they took) on grounds that had nothing to do with cultural freedom. They condemned vigilantism on the grounds that it embarrassed the United States abroad and interfered with the government's efforts to root out the communist conspiracy at home. They criticized interference with art not because they thought that the best art inevitably subverts conventions (including political ones) and is valuable for that very reason but because they believed, on the contrary, that art and politics should be "divorced."[7] They defended academic freedom for noncommunists only, and even for noncommunists they defended it on the ground that educators,

[6] Ibid., September 18, 1955.
[7] The popularity of the "new criticism," with its insistence that a work of art can be understood without any reference to external events, was symptomatic of the cultural climate of the fifties.

as experts in a complicated technique, ought to be left alone to manage their own affairs. In all of this, the cold-war intellectuals revealed themselves as the servants of bureaucratic power; and it was not altogether surprising, years later, to find that the relation of intellectuals to power was even closer than it had seemed at the time. The history of the fifties had already shown that intellectuals were unusually sensitive to their interests as a group and that they defined those interests in such a way as to make them fully compatible with the interests of the state. As a group, intellectuals had achieved a semiofficial status which assigned them professional responsibility for the machinery of education and for cultural affairs in general. Within this sphere—within the schools, the universities, the theater, the concert hall, and the politico-literary magazines—they had achieved both autonomy and affluence, as the social value of their services became apparent to the government, to corporations, and to the foundations. Professional intellectuals had become indispensable to society and to the state (in ways which neither the intellectuals nor even the state always perceived), partly because of the increasing importance of education—especially the need for trained experts —and partly because the cold war seemed to demand that the United States compete with communism in the cultural sphere as well as in every other. The modern state, among other things, is an engine of propaganda, alternately manufacturing crises and claiming to be the only instrument that can effectively deal with them. This propaganda, in order to be successful, demands the cooperation of writers, teachers, and artists not as paid propagandists or state-censored timeservers but as "free" intellectuals capable of policing their own jurisdictions and of enforcing acceptable standards of responsibility within the various intellectual professions.

A system like this presupposes two things: a high degree

of professional consciousness among intellectuals, and general economic affluence which frees the patrons of intellectual life from the need to account for the money they spend on culture. Once these conditions exist, as they have existed in the United States for some time, intellectuals can be trusted to censor themselves, and crude "political" influence over intellectual life comes to seem passé. In the Soviet Union, on the other hand, intellectuals are insufficiently professionalized to be able effectively to resist political control. As one would expect in a developing society, a strong commitment to applied knowledge mitigates against the development of "pure" standards, which is one of the chief prerequisites of professionalization. It can be demonstrated that in the nineteenth century United States professionalization of intellectual activities went hand in hand with the acceptance of pure research as a legitimate enterprise, first among intellectuals themselves and then among their patrons.[8] Only when they win acceptance for pure research do intellectuals establish themselves as masters in their own house, free from the nagging public scrutiny that naively expects to see the value of intellectual activity measured in immediate practical applications. This battle having been won, the achievement of "academic freedom" is comparatively easy, since academic freedom presents itself (as we have seen) not as a defense of the necessarily subversive character of good intellectual work, but as a prerequisite for pure research. Moreover, the more intellectual purity identifies itself with "value-free" investigations, the more it empties itself of political content and the easier it is for public officials to tolerate it. The "scientific" spirit, spreading from the natural sciences to social studies, tends to

[8] George H. Daniels: "The Pure-Science Ideal and Democratic Culture," *Science*, June 30, 1967, pp. 1699–705.

drain the latter of their critical potential while at the same time making them ideal instruments of bureaucratic control.

Pure science, once it comes to dominate the organized life of the intellect, paradoxically establishes itself as even more useful to the prevailing social order than the practical knowledge it displaces—useful, if not in the immediate present, in the not-too-distant future. The high status enjoyed by American intellectuals depends on their having convinced their backers in government and industry that "basic research" produces better results in the long run than mindless empiricism. But in order for intellectuals to win this battle it was necessary not only to convince themselves of these things but to overcome the narrowly utilitarian approach to knowledge that usually prevails among the patrons of learning. The advancement of pure learning on a large scale demands that the sponsors of learning be willing to spend large sums of money without hope of immediate return. In advanced capitalism, this requirement happily coincides with the capitalists' need to engage in conspicuous expenditure; hence the dominant role played by "captains of industry" in the professionalization of higher education (with the results described by Veblen in *The Higher Learning in America*).

At a still later stage of development, the same role is played by the foundations and directly by government, both of which need to engage in a form of expenditure (not necessarily conspicuous in all its details) that shares with the conspicuous expenditure of the capitalist a marked indifference to results. Modern bureaucracies are money-spending agencies. The more money a bureaucracy can spend, the larger the budget it can claim. Since the bureaucracy is more interested in its own aggrandizement than in doing a job, the bureaucrat is restrained in his expenditure only by the need to account to some superior and ultimately, perhaps, to the public; but in complicated bureaucracies it is hard for anyone to account for the money, particularly since a state of continual emergency can be invoked to justify secrecy in all the important operations of government. This state of perfect nonaccountability, which is the goal toward which bureaucracies ceaselessly strive, works to the indirect advantage of pure research and of the professionalized intellectuals.

In Soviet Russia, a comparatively undeveloped economy cannot sustain the luxury of unaccounted expenditure, and the bureaucracy is still infected, therefore, by a penny-pinching mentality that begrudges expenditures unless they can be justified in utilitarian terms. This attitude, together with the lack of professional consciousness among intellectuals themselves (many of whom share the belief that knowledge is valuable not for itself but for the social and political uses to which it can be put), is the source of the political interference with knowledge that is so widely deplored in the West. It is obvious that the critical spirit cannot thrive under these conditions. Even art is judged in narrowly utilitarian terms and subjected to autocratic regulation by ignorant bureaucrats. What needs to be emphasized, however, is that the triumph of academic freedom in the United States, under the special conditions which have brought it about, does not necessarily lead to intellectual independence and critical thinking. It is a serious mistake to confuse academic freedom with cultural freedom. American intellectuals are not subject to political controls but the very conditions which have brought about this result have undermined their capacity for independent thought. The American press is free, but it censors itself. The university is free, but it has purged itself of ideas. The literary intellectuals are free, but they use their freedom to propagandize for the state.

The freedom of American intellectuals as a professional class blinds them to their un-freedom. It leads them to confuse the political interests of intellectuals as an official minority with the progress of intellect. Their freedom from overt political control (particularly from "vigilantes") blinds them to the way in which the "knowledge industry" has been incorporated into the state and the military-industrial complex. Since the state exerts so little censorship over the cultural enterprises it subsidizes—since on the contrary it supports basic research, congresses for cultural freedom, and various liberal organizations—intellectuals do not see that these activities serve the interests of the state, not the interests of intellect. All they can see is the absence of external censorship; that and that alone proves to their satisfaction that Soviet intellectuals are slaves and American intellectuals free men. Meanwhile their own self-censorship makes them eligible for the official recognition and support that sustain the illusion that the American government, unlike the Soviet government, greatly values the life of the mind. The circle of illusion is thus complete; and even the revelation that the campaign for "cultural freedom" was itself the creation and tool of the state has not yet torn away the veil.

[VII]

That there is no necessary contradiction between the interests of organized intellectuals and the interests of American world power, that the intellectual community can be trusted to police itself and should be left free from annoying pressures from outside, that dissenting opinion within the framework of agreement on cold-war fundamentals not only should be tolerated but can be turned to effective propaganda use abroad—all these things were apparent in the early fifties to the more enlightened members of the governmental bureaucracy; but they were far from being universally acknowledged even in the bureaucracy, much less in Congress or in the country as a whole. "Back in the early 1950's," says Thomas W. Braden, the man who supervised the cultural activities of the CIA, ". . . the idea that Congress would have approved many of our projects was about as likely as the John Birch Society's approving Medicare."[9] There was resistance to these projects in the CIA itself. To a man of Braden's background and inclinations the idea of supporting liberal and socialist "fronts" grew naturally out of the logic of the cold war. During the Second World War Braden served with the OSS—next to the communist movement itself the most fruitful source, it would appear, of postwar anticommunism (the same people often having served in both). Before joining the CIA in 1950, Braden taught English at Dartmouth and served for two years as executive secretary of the Museum of Modern Art; later he became president of the California Board of Education, where he defended a liberal view of academic freedom against those who wished to ban J. D. Salinger's *The Catcher in the Rye* from school libraries. Braden was a new type of bureaucrat, equally at home in government and in academic circles; but when in 1950 he proposed that "the CIA ought to take on the Russians by penetrating a battery of international fronts," his

---

[9] Thomas W. Braden: "I'm Glad the CIA Is 'Immoral,'" *Saturday Evening Post*, May 20, 1967, p. 10. On Braden see *The New York Times*, May 8, 1967.

more conventional colleagues made the quaint objection that "this is just another one of those goddamned proposals for getting into everybody's hair." Allan Dulles intervened to save the project after it had been voted down by the division chiefs. "Thus began the first centralized effort to combat Communist fronts."[1]

Before they had finished, the directors of the CIA had infiltrated the National Student Association, the Institute of International Labor Research, the American Newspaper Guild, the American Friends of the Middle East, the National Council of Churches, and many other worthy organizations.[2] "We . . . placed one agent in a Europe-based organization of intellectuals called the Congress for Cultural Freedom," Braden notes.[3] This "agent" was Michael Josselson, who was born in Russia in 1908, educated in Germany, represented American department stores in Paris in the mid-thirties, came to the United States just before the war, and was naturalized in 1941. During the war Josselson, like Braden, served in the OSS. Afterwards he was sent to Berlin as an officer for cultural affairs in Patton's army. There he met Melvin J. Lasky. When they organized the Congress for Cultural Freedom in 1950, Josselson became its executive director.[4]

---

[1] Braden: "I'm Glad the CIA Is 'Immoral,' " p. 12.

[2] On the CIA's cultural activities see *The New York Times*, April 27, 1966; St. Louis *Post-Dispatch*, February 19, 1967; Chicago *Sun-Times*, February 14, 15, 22, 23, 30, 1967; *Christian Science Monitor*, March 10, 1967; Andrew Kopkind: "CIA: The Great Corrupter," *New Statesman*, February 24, 1967, pp. 249–50; Jason Epstein: "The CIA and the Intellectuals," *New York Review of Books*, April 20, 1967, pp. 16–21; Sol Stern: "A Short Account of International Student Politics & the Cold War," *Ramparts*, March 1967, pp. 29–38.

[3] Braden: "I'm Glad the CIA Is 'Immoral,' " p. 12.

[4] *The New York Times*, May 15, 1967.

"Another agent became an editor of *Encounter.*"[5] The usefulness of these agents, Braden comments, was that they "could not only propose anti-Communist programs to the official leaders of the organizations but they could also suggest ways and means to solve the inevitable budgetary problems. Why not see if the needed money could be obtained from 'American foundations'?"[6] Note that he does not describe the role of the CIA as having been restricted to financing these fronts; its agents were also to promote "anti-Communist programs." When it became public that the Congress for Cultural Freedom had been financed for sixteen years by the CIA, the editors of *Encounter* made a great point of the fact that the congress had never dictated policy to the magazine; but the whole question takes on a different color in light of Braden's disclosure that one of the editors worked for the CIA. Under these circumstances, it was unnecessary for the congress to dictate policy to *Encounter;* nor would the other editors, ignorant of these connections, have been aware of any direct intervention by the CIA.

[5] Braden: "I'm Glad the CIA Is 'Immoral,'" p. 12. "Braden's allegation was untrue," Melvin J. Lasky contends. (*The Nation,* October 2, 1967, p. 309.) In a subsequent statement, he argues, Braden "in effect withdrew" his allegation when he explained that "by an 'agent,'" in Lasky's words, "he also meant 'unwitting' persons." The article to which Lasky refers (*The New York Times,* May 8, 1967) reads: "Mr. Braden refused to name the CIA 'agents' in the congress or the magazine, nor would he describe what kind of agents he meant. The agency, he said, used the term 'agent' to describe both 'witting' and 'unwitting' operatives. But the article in *The Saturday Evening Post* clearly implies that the persons involved were 'agents' before they were 'placed' in the congress and 'became an editor' of *Encounter.*" I see nothing in this report that entitles the reader to conclude that Braden "in effect withdrew" his earlier statement.

[6] Braden: "I'm Glad the CIA Is 'Immoral,'" p. 12.

On April 27, 1966, *The New York Times,* in a long article on the CIA, reported that the CIA had supported the Congress for Cultural Freedom and other organizations through a system of dummy foundations, and that *"Encounter* magazine . . . was for a long time—though it is not now—one of the indirect beneficiaries of C.I.A. funds." (Rumors to this effect had circulated for years.) The editors of *Encounter*—Stephen Spender, Lasky, and Irving Kristol—wrote an extremely disingenuous letter to the *Times* in which they tried to refute the assertion without denying it outright.[7] They asserted—what was a half-truth at best—that the congress's funds "were derived from various recognized foundations—all of them (from such institutions as the Ford and Rockefeller foundations to the smaller ones) publicly listed in the official directories."[8] What was not publicly listed, of course, was the fact that some of these "smaller ones" received money from the CIA for the express purpose of supporting the Congress for Cultural Freedom. Thus between 1961 and 1966, the CIA through some of its phony foundations gave $430,700 to the Hoblitzelle Foundation, a philanthropical enterprise established by the Dallas millionaire Karl Hoblitzelle, and the Hoblitzelle Foundation obligingly passed along these funds to the Congress for Cultural Freedom.[9] Needless to say, no hint of these transactions appeared in the Lasky-Spender-Kristol letter to the *Times.*

Privately, Lasky went much further and declared cate-

---

[7] Spender, Kristol, and Frank Kermode all insist that they knew nothing of *Encounter*'s relations with the CIA until the matter became public, Lasky having assured them that there was nothing to the persistent rumors they had heard.

[8] *The New York Times,* May 10, 1966.

[9] Ibid., February 19, March 10, May 10, 1967; *Newsweek,* March 6, 1967, p. 31.

gorically that *Encounter* had never received funds from the CIA. (Later he admitted that he had been "insufficiently frank" with his colleagues and friends.[1]) In public, however, the magazine's defense was conducted in language of deliberate ambiguity. Another letter to the *Times,* signed by John Kenneth Galbraith, George Kennan, Robert Oppenheimer, and Arthur Schlesinger, Jr., completely avoided the question of *Encounter*'s financing and argued merely that the magazine's editorial independence proved that it had never been "used" by the CIA—a statement, however, which carried with it the implication that the CIA had had nothing to do with the organization at all.[2] One must ask why these men felt it necessary to make such a guarded statement, and why, since they had to state their position so cautiously, they felt it necessary to make any statement at all. The matter is even more puzzling in view of Galbraith's statement in the New York *World Journal Tribune* that "some years ago," while attending a meeting of the congress in Berlin (he probably refers to a conference held there in 1960), he had been told by a "knowledgeable friend" that the Congress for Cultural Freedom might be receiving support from the CIA. Galbraith says that he "subjected its treasurer to interrogation and found that the poor fellow had been trained in ambiguity but not dissemblance." "I was disturbed," he says, "and I don't think I would have attended any more meetings" if his entrance into government service had not ended his participation.[3] In another interview Galbraith told Ivan Yates of the London *Observer* that he "made a mental note to attend no more meetings of the Congress." Yates asked "how in that case he

---

[1] *The New York Times,* May 9, 1967.
[2] Ibid., May 9, 1966.
[3] New York *World Journal Tribune,* March 13, 1967.

could possibly have signed the letter to *The New York Times*. He replied that at the time, he had 'very strong suspicions' that the CIA had been financing the Congress. 'I was writing really with reference to *Encounter,* but you could easily persuade me that the letter was much too fulsome.' "[4]

Whereas Lasky believes that he was "insufficiently frank," Galbraith allows that he may have been "too fulsome." His urbanity is imperturbable. The letter was "fulsome" indeed. Moreover, it specifically dealt with the Congress for Cultural Freedom, not with *Encounter,* which it does not even mention by name. The letter states that "examination of the record of the congress, its magazines and its other activities will, we believe, convince the most skeptical that the congress has had no loyalty except an unswerving commitment to cultural freedom. . . ." Yet one of the signers of this statement was sufficiently skeptical to have "made a mental note" not to attend any more meetings of the congress! And he was assuring the still unsuspecting public of the congress's unimpeachable independence long after he had privately reached the conclusion that it was probably being supported by the CIA.

We have heard a great deal about the "credibility gap" that is supposed to have been created by the Johnson Administration; but what about the credibility of our most eminent intellectuals? As a further indication of the values that prevail among them, when the *Encounter* affair finally became public, Galbraith's principal concern was that a valuable public enterprise was in danger of being discredited. The whole wretched business seemed inescapably to point to the conclusion that cultural freedom had been consistently confused with American propaganda, and that

[4] London *Observer,* May 14, 1967.

"cultural freedom," as defined by its leading defenders, was—to put it bluntly—a hoax. Yet at precisely the moment when the dimensions of the hoax were fully revealed, Galbraith joined the congress's board of directors; and "I intend," he said, "to put some extra effort into its activities. I think this is the right course and I would urge similar effort on behalf of other afflicted but reformed organizations."[5]

What should a "free thinker" do, asks the *Sunday Times* of London, "when he finds out that his free thought has been subsidized by a ruthlessly aggressive intelligence agency as part of the international cold war?"[6] According to the curious values that prevail in American society, he should make a redoubled effort to salvage the reputation of organizations that have been compromised, it would seem, beyond redemption. Far from "reforming" themselves— even assuming that this was possible—*Encounter* and the Congress for Cultural Freedom have vindicated the very men who led them into disaster. At their meeting in Paris last May, officials of the congress voted to keep Josselson in his post.[7] Likewise, the management of *Encounter* gave Lasky "a vote of confidence."[8]

Ever since *The New York Times* asserted that *Encounter* had been subsidized by the CIA, the congress and its defenders have tried to brazen out the crisis by intimidating their critics—the same tactics that worked so well in the days of the cold war. Arthur Schlesinger leaped into the breach by attacking one of *Encounter*'s principal critics,

---

[5] New York *World Journal Tribune*, March 13, 1967.

[6] London *Sunday Times*, May 14, 1967.

[7] Alexander Werth: "Literary Bay of Pigs," *The Nation*, June 5, 1967, pp. 710–11. Eventually he was replaced by Shepard Stone; *The New York Times*, October 3, 1967.

[8] Ibid., May 9, 1967.

Conor Cruise O'Brien. Following the *Times*'s initial disclosures, O'Brien delivered a lecture at New York University,[9] subsequently published in *Book Week,* in which he referred to the *Times*'s story and went on to observe that "the beauty of the [CIA-*Encounter*] operation . . . was that writers of the first rank, who had no interest at all in serving the power structure, were induced to do so unwittingly," while "the writing specifically required by the power structure" could be done by writers of lesser ability, men skilled in public relations and "who were, as the Belgians used to say about Moise Tshombe, *compréhensifs,* that is, they could take a hint."[1] In reply, Schlesinger at first dodged the question of *Encounter*'s relations with the CIA by attacking O'Brien's "apparent inability to conceive any reason for opposition to communism except bribery by the CIA." When pressed, he said that "so long as I have been a member of the *Encounter* Trust, *Encounter* has not been the beneficiary, direct or indirect, of CIA funds."[2] (The subsidies to *Encounter*, it is now known, ran from 1953 to 1964, although the congress's connection with the CIA, according to Galbraith, continued until 1966.[3]) Moreover, Schlesinger said, Spender, Lasky, and Kristol had revealed "the past sources of *Encounter*'s support" and documented "its editorial and political independence."[4] They had of course, done nothing of the kind. The magazine's editorial

[9] "The Writer and the Power Structure," Homer Watt Lecture, May 19, 1966.

[1] *Book Week,* June 12, 1966; see also Conor Cruise O'Brien: "Some Encounters with the Culturally Free," *Rights,* spring 1967, p. 4.

[2] *Book Week,* September 11, 1966, p. 6.

[3] New York *World Journal Tribune,* March 13, 1967.

[4] *Book Week,* September 11, 1966, p. 6.

independence was not to be taken on the editors' word, and the question of its financing was an issue they had studiously avoided. Why did Schlesinger go out of his way to endorse their evasions? Presumably he knew as much about *Encounter*'s relations with the CIA as Galbraith— probably a good deal more. How was cultural freedom served by lending oneself to a deliberate deception?

In August 1966 *Encounter* published a scurrilous attack on O'Brien by "R" (Goronwy Rees). O'Brien's allegations against *Encounter,* according to "R," were evidence of "the degeneration of a literary critic" into a "Joe McCarthy of politico-cultural criticism, hunting for CIA agents beneath the beds of Stephen Spender, Irving Kristol, Melvin Lasky, and Frank Kermode." An "air of bad faith combined with moral elevation . . . impregnate[d]" O'Brien's work.[5] Karl Miller of the *New Statesman* offered O'Brien space to reply, but when Frank Kermode of *Encounter* learned of this, he called Miller and threatened to sue the *New Statesman* for libel if O'Brien's piece contained any reference to *Encounter*'s relations with the CIA.[6] O'Brien then sued *Encounter* and won a judgment in Ireland. At this point, *Ramparts* broke the story of the CIA's infiltration of the National Student Association, bringing a whole series of other disclosures in its wake, including the CIA's connection with the Congress for Cultural Freedom. The editors of *Encounter,* unable to deny those relations any longer, and threatened with heavy damages, apologized to O'Brien, retracted their aspersions on his integrity, which they now ad-

---

[5] *Encounter*, August 1966, pp. 41, 43.

[6] O'Brien: "Some Encounters with the Culturally Free," pp. 4–5. It is interesting to note that Lasky was out of the country when the other editors of *Encounter* decided to file suit against O'Brien.

mitted were "without justification," and agreed to pay his legal expenses.[7]

Throughout this controversy, the editors of *Encounter* repeatedly pointed to their editorial independence, first in order to deny (by implication) any connection with the CIA, and then when it was impossible any longer to deny that, in order to prove that the CIA, although supporting the magazine, had not tried to dictate its editorial policy—or in Josselson's words, that the money had "never, never" been used "for propaganda and intelligence purposes."[8] Spender, Kristol, and Lasky, in their letter to the *Times,* claimed that "we are our own masters and are part of nobody's propaganda."[9] The letter signed by Galbraith and Schlesinger declared that *Encounter* maintained "no loyalty except an unswerving commitment to cultural freedom" and that it had "freely criticized actions and policies of all nations, including the United States."[1] These statements, however, need to be set against Thomas Braden's account of the rules that guided the international organization of the CIA: "Use legitimate, existing organizations; disguise the extent of American interest; protect the integrity of the organization by not requiring it to support every aspect of official American policy."[2]

These rules do more than shed light on the nature and extent of *Encounter*'s editorial freedom. By publishing them at a time when they must surely have embarrassed the writers concerned, Braden revealed a contempt for their kept intellectuals which the officers of the CIA could not conceal. Whatever the intellectuals may have thought of the relation-

[7] Ibid., pp. 5–7.
[8] Werth: "Literary Bay of Pigs," p. 711.
[9] *The New York Times,* May 10, 1966.
[1] Ibid., May 9, 1966.
[2] Braden: "I'm Glad the CIA is 'Immoral,'" p. 14.

ship, the CIA regarded them exactly as the Communist party regarded its fronts in the thirties and forties—as instruments of its own purpose.[3] Most of the beneficiaries of the CIA have been understandably slow to see this point; it is hard to admit that one has been used and that one's sense of freedom and power is an illusion. Norman Thomas, for instance, admits that he should have known where the money for his Institute of International Labor Relations was coming from, but (like Galbraith, like Thomas Braden himself) what he chiefly regrets is that a worthwhile work has had to come prematurely to an end. The Kaplan Fund, Thomas insists, "never interfered in any way"—which merely means that he was never aware of its interference.[4] He does not see that he was being used, as Stephen Spender puts it in his own case, "for quite different purposes" from the ones he thought he was advancing.[5] *He* thought he was working for democratic reform in Latin America, whereas the CIA valued him as a showpiece, an anticommunist who happened to be a socialist.[6]

Spender has had the wit to recognize the situation for what it was. "In reality," he writes, the intellectuals employed by the CIA without their knowledge were "being

---

[3] "The CIA experience, for most of my friends who engaged in it directly, was, I suspect, very like what the experience of being a Communist must have been for many other Americans." Murray Kempton in *Commentary,* September 1967, p. 53.

[4] *The New York Times,* February 22, 1967.

[5] Ibid., March 27, 1967.

[6] Braden is under the impression that this combination was almost irresistible to Europeans, at whom the CIA's cultural program was directed. "The fact, of course, is that in much of Europe in the 1950's, socialists, people who called themselves 'left'—the very people whom many Americans thought no better than Communists—were the only people who gave a damn about fighting Communism." Braden: "I'm Glad the CIA Is 'Immoral,'" p. 10.

used for concealed government propaganda." Spencer admits that this arrangement made a "mockery" of intellectual freedom.[7] Michael Wood, formerly of the NSA, has written even more poignantly of his relations with the world of power. "Those of us who worked for NSA during 1965–1966, experienced an unusual sense of personal liberation. While actively involved in many of the insurgent campus and political movements of the day, we were also able to move freely through the highest echelons of established power." These experiences, Wood says, "gave us a heady feeling and a sense of power beyond our years." But "to learn that it had been bought with so terrible a compromise made me realize how impotent we really were."[8]

[VIII]

What conclusions can be drawn from the history of the cultural cold war? Some should be obvious. Thanks to the revelations of the CIA's secret subsidies, it is no longer a very novel or startling proposition to say that American officials have committed themselves to fighting fire with fire, and that this strategy is self-defeating because the means corrupt the end. "In our attempts to fight unscrupulous opponents," asks Arthur J. Moore in *Christianity and Crisis,* "have we ended up debauching ourselves?"[9] The history of the cold war makes it clear that the question can only be answered with an emphatic affirmative.

These events, if people consider them seriously and try to confront their implications without flinching, will lead

[7] *The New York Times,* March 27, 1967.
[8] *Ramparts,* March 1967, p. 38.
[9] *Christianity and Crisis,* May 29, 1967, p. 117.

many Americans to question (perhaps for the first time) the cant about American "pluralism," the "open society," etc. Andrew Kopkind puts it very well: "The illusion of dissent was maintained: the CIA supported Socialist cold warriors, Fascist cold warriors, black and white cold warriors. . . . But it was a sham pluralism, and it was utterly corrupting."[1] A society which tolerates an illusory dissent is in much greater danger, in some respects, than a society in which uniformity is ruthlessly imposed.

For twenty years Americans have been told that their country is an open society and that communist peoples live in slavery. Now it appears that the very men who were most active in spreading this gospel were themselves the servants ("witty" in some cases, unsuspecting in others) of the secret police. The whole show—the youth congresses, the cultural congresses, the trips abroad, the great glamorous display of American freedom and American civilization and the American standard of living—was all arranged behind the scenes by men who believed, with Thomas Braden, that "the cold war was and is a war, fought with ideas instead of bombs."[2] Men who have never been able to conceive of ideas as anything but instruments of national power were the sponsors of "cultural freedom."

The revelations about the intellectuals and the CIA should also make it easier to understand a point about the relation of intellectuals to power that has been widely misunderstood. In associating themselves with the war-making and propaganda machinery of the state in the hope of influencing it, intellectuals deprive themselves of the real influence they could have as men who refuse to judge the validity of ideas by the requirements of national power or any

---

[1] *New Statesman*, February 24, 1967, p. 249.
[2] Braden: "I'm Glad the CIA Is 'Immoral,' " p. 14.

other entrenched interest. Time after time in this century it has been shown that the dream of influencing the war machine is a delusion. Instead the war machine corrupts the intellectuals. The war machine cannot be influenced by the advice of well-meaning intellectuals in the inner councils of government; it can only be resisted. The way to resist it is simply to refuse to put oneself at its service. That does not mean playing at revolution; it does not mean putting on blackface and adopting the speech of the ghetto; it does not mean turning on, tuning in, and dropping out; it does not even mean engaging in desperate acts of conscience which show one's willingness to take risks and to undergo physical danger. Masked as a higher selflessness, these acts become self-serving, having as their object not truth nor even social change but the promotion of the individual's self-esteem. Moreover they betray, at a deeper level, the same loss of faith which drives others into the service of the men in power—a haunting suspicion that history belongs to men of action and that men of ideas are powerless in a world that has no use for philosophy.

It is precisely this belief that has enabled the same men in one lifetime to serve both the Communist party and the CIA in the delusion that they were helping to make history —only to find, in both cases, that all they had made was a lie. But these defeats—the revelation that the man of action, revolutionist or bureaucrat, scorns the philosopher whom he is able to use—have not led the philosopher to conclude that he should not allow himself to be used; they merely reinforce his self-contempt and make him the ready victim of a new political cause.

The despair of intellect is closely related to the despair of democracy. In our time intellectuals are fascinated by conspiracy and intrigue, even as they celebrate the "free marketplace of ideas" (itself an expression that already betrays a tendency to regard ideas as commodities). They long to be on the inside of things; they want to share the secrets ordinary people are not permitted to hear.

In the last twenty years, the elitism of intellectuals has expressed itself as a celebration of American life, and this fact makes it hard to see the continuity between the thirties and forties on the one hand and the fifties and sixties on the other. The hyper-Americanism of the latter period seems to be a reaction against the anti-Americanism of the depression years. Both of these phenomena, however, spring from the same source, the intellectuals' disenchantment with democracy and their alienation from intellect itself. Intellectuals associate themselves with the American war machine not so much because it represents America as because it represents action, power, and conspiracy; and the identification is even easier because the war machine is itself "alienated" from the people it claims to defend. The defense intellectuals, cool and arrogant, pursue their obscure calculations in a little world bounded by the walls of the Pentagon, sealed off from the difficult reality outside which does not always respond to their formulas and which, therefore, has to be ignored in arriving at correct solutions to the "problems" of government. At Langley, Virginia, the CIA turns its back on America and busies itself with its empire abroad. But this empire, which the CIA tries to police, has no relation to the real lives of the people of the world—it is a fantasy of the CIA, in which conspiracy and counter-conspiracy, freedom and communist slavery, the forces of light and the forces of darkness, are locked in timeless combat. The concrete embodiments of these abstractions have long since ceased to matter. The processes of government have been intellectualized. Albert D. Biderman, the prophet of "social accounting," speaks for the dominant ethos: "With the growth of the complexity of society, immediate experience with its events plays an increasingly smaller role as a source of information and basis of judgment in contrast to symbolically mediated information about these events. . . . Numerical indexes of phenomena are peculiarly fitted to these needs."[3]

Washington belongs to the "future-planners," men who believe that "social accounting" will solve social "problems." Government is a "think tank," an ivory tower, a community of scholars. A member of the RAND Corporation speaks of its "academic freedom" which "allows you to think about what you want to." A civil servant praises the democratic tolerance, the respect for ideas, that prevails in the Defense Department. Herman Kahn, jolly, avuncular, encourages "intellectual diversity"; on his staff at the Hudson Institute, a center of learning devoted to the science of systematic destruction, he retains a dedicated pacifist who doubtless thinks that he is slowly converting the Hudson Institute to universal brotherhood.[4]

Never before have the ruling classes been so solicitous of cultural freedom; but since this freedom no longer has anything to do with "immediate experience and its events," it exists in a decontaminated void.

[3] Sol Stern: "The Defense Intellectuals," *Ramparts*, February 1967, pp. 32–7; Andrew Kopkind: "The Future Planners," *New Republic*, February 25, 1967, p. 19.

[4] *Ramparts*, February 1967, pp. 33, 32.

CHAPTER FOUR

BLACK POWER: CULTURAL NATIONALISM AS POLITICS

In the place of a matured social vision there will always be those who will gladly substitute the catastrophic and glorious act of martyrdom and self-immolation for a cause.
—Harold Cruse, *The Crisis of the Negro Intellectual*

WHATEVER ELSE "BLACK POWER" MEANS, THE SLOGAN itself indicates that the movement for racial equality has entered a new phase. Even those who argue that the change is largely rhetorical or that Black Power merely complements the struggle for "civil rights" would presumably not deny that "Black Power" articulates, at the very least, a new sense of urgency, if not a sense of impending crisis. Together with the riots, it challenges the belief, until recently widespread, that the United States is making substantial progress toward racial justice and that it is only a matter of time and further effort before the color line is effectively obliterated.

Now even the opponents of Black Power issue warnings of apocalypse. "We shall overcome" no longer expresses the spirit of the struggle. Race war seems a more likely prospect. The Negro movement itself is splitting along racial lines. In the form in which it existed until 1963 or 1964, the civil rights movement is dead: this is not a conjecture but a historical fact. Whether the movement can be revived in some other form, or whether it will give way to something completely different, remains to be seen. Meanwhile time seems to be working on the side of an imminent disaster.

What has changed? Why did the civil rights movement, which seemed so confident and successful at the time of the Washington march in 1963, falter until now it seems to have reached the point of collapse? Why has "Black Power" displaced "freedom" as the rallying-point of Negro militancy?

Several things have happened. The most obvious is that the apparent victories of the civil rights coalition have not brought about any discernible changes in the lives of most Negroes, at least not in the north. Almost all commentators on Black Power acknowledge this failure or insist on it, depending on the point of view. Charles E. Fager, for example, analyzes in detail the Civil Rights Act of 1964—the major legislative achievement of the civil rights coalition—and shows how the act has been systematically subverted in the South, title by title, and how, in the North, many of its provisions (such as voting safeguards and desegregation of public accommodations) were irrelevant to begin with.[1] The inadequacy of civil rights legislation is not difficult to grasp. Even the most superficial accounts of the riots in Newark and Detroit see the connection between hopes raised by civil rights agitation and the Negroes' disappointing realization that this agitation, whatever its apparent successes, has nevertheless failed to relieve the tangible miseries of ghetto life.[2]

Not only have the civil rights laws proved to be intrinsically weaker and more limited in their application than they seemed at the time they were passed, but the unexpectedly

---

[1] Charles E. Fager: *White Reflections on Black Power* (Grand Rapids: William B. Eerdmans; 1967), pp. 62–7.

[2] The best study of a riot is Tom Hayden: "The Occupation of Newark," *New York Review of Books*, August 24, 1967, pp. 14–24.

bitter resistance to civil rights, particularly in the North, has made it difficult to implement even these limited gains, let alone to win new struggles for open housing, an end to de facto segregation, and equal employment. Northern segregationists may not be strong enough to elect Mrs. Louise Day Hicks mayor of Boston, but they can delay open housing indefinitely, it would seem, in Milwaukee as well as in every other Northern city—even those which have nominally adopted open housing. Everywhere in the North civil rights agitation, instead of breaking down barriers as expected, has met a wall of resistance. If anything, Negroes have made more gains in the South than in the North. The strategy of the civil rights movement, resting implicitly on the premise that the North was more enlightened than the South, was unprepared for the resistance it has encountered in the North.

The shifting focus of the struggle from the South to the North thus has contributed both to the weakening of the civil rights movement and to the emergence of Black Power. The implications of this change of scene go beyond what is immediately evident—that federal troops, for instance, appear on the side of the Negroes in Little Rock, whereas in Detroit they are the enemy. The civil rights movement in the South was the product of a set of conditions which is not likely to be repeated in the North: federal efforts to "reconstruct" the South; the tendency of Northern liberals to express their distaste for American society vicariously by attacking racism in the South, rather than by confronting racism at home; the revival of Southern liberalism. Moreover, the civil rights movement, in its Southern phase, rested on the indigenous Negro subculture which has grown up since the Civil War under the peculiar conditions of Southern segregation—a culture separate and unequal but semiautonomous and therefore capable of giving its own distinctive character to the movement for legal and political equality.

E. Franklin Frazier once wrote that the black man's "primary struggle" in America "has been to acquire a culture"—customs, values, and forms of expression which, transmitted from generation to generation, provide a people with a sense of its own integrity and collective identity.[3] Under slavery, African forms of social organization, family life, religion, language, and even art disintegrated, leaving the slave neither an African nor an American but a man suspended, as Kenneth Stampp has said, "between two cultures," unable to participate in either.[4] A few scholars, notably Melville J. Herskovits in *The Myth of the Negro Past,* have argued that African culture survived and became the basis of Negro culture in the New World. Much of Herskovits's famous study concerns itself, however, with refuting stereotypes of Negro inferiority which by the author's own admission are "not to be taken seriously."[5] The destruction of these clichés proves nothing, one way or the other, about the survival of African culture in the New World. In a chapter on "The Search for Tribal Origins," Herskovits tries to prove that slaves were taken "from a far more restricted area than had been thought the case" and that therefore they spoke the same language and shared common cultural patterns.[6] Much of the data presented, how-

---

[3] E. Franklin Frazier: "La Bourgeoisie Noir," *Modern Quarterly,* 1929; quoted in Harold Cruse: *The Crisis of the Negro Intellectual* (New York: William Morrow; 1967), p. 154.

[4] Kenneth Stampp: *The Peculiar Institution* (New York: Alfred A. Knopf; 1956), Ch. viii.

[5] Melville J. Herskovits: *The Myth of the Negro Past* (Boston: Beacon Press; 1958 [New York, 1941]), p. 24.

[6] Ibid., p. 33.

ever, reveals only the place of export and tells us nothing about tribal origins. And although Herskovits shows that West African languages may have shared certain features, this does not prove that they were mutually intelligible; and in any case the fact remains that in the New World African languages quickly gave way to European dialects.[7] In another chapter Herskovits tries to make a connection between West African polygyny and the matricentric Negro family in the New World; but the latter is now generally recognized as a distinctive form of family organization bearing no resemblance to polygyny—a fact which Herskovits explicitly admits: "It goes without saying that the plantation system rendered the survival of African family types impossible."[8] On the crucial question of what effect contact with whites had on African culture, Herskovits's argument is internally inconsistent. At one point he argues that greater contact between blacks and whites in the South, vis-à-vis Latin America, explains why fewer Africanisms survived in the South than elsewhere; but when he turns to Latin America, he maintains that "mere contact" did not bring about "the supression of Africanisms."[9] Finally, Herskovits himself admits that African culture played a negligible role in the American South.

The one thing that emerges clearly from Herskovits's work is that whether one is talking about Latin America or about the United States, African survivals are easier to trace in areas like music and religion than in language, politics, social organization, and family life, where they seem almost nonexistent.

Unfortunately the whole question of African survivals

[7] Ibid., p. 295.
[8] Ibid., pp. 64, 169 ff., 139.
[9] Ibid., pp. 120, 125.

has now become involved in the politics of cultural nationalism, and it is hard to argue against Herskovits without being accused of wishing to subvert the cultural identity of black people. Herskovits himself explicitly acknowledged a desire "to give the Negro an appreciation of his past" and "to endow him with the confidence in his own position in this country and in the world which he must have."[1] The same purpose animates many of his present admirers. It is no service to black nationalism, however, to pretend that it grows out of an African heritage; nor is it even necessary to the argument that Negro culture in America ought to be preserved. If the defense of that culture rested only on appeals to the African past, it would not be worth defending.

American Negro culture grew not out of African survivals nor even out of the legacy of slavery but out of the experience of the Negro people in the South after the Civil War. After emancipation, Southern Negroes gradually developed institutions of their own, derived from American sources but adapted to their own needs, and therefore capable of giving the Negro community the beginnings at least of cohesiveness and collective self-discipline. The Negro church managed to impose strict standards of sexual morality, thereby making possible the emergence of stable families over which the father—not the mother, as under slavery—presided.[2]

Stable families, in turn, furnished the continuity between generations without which Negroes could not even have begun their slow and painful self-advancement—the accumulation of talent, skills, and leadership which by the

---

[1] Ibid., p. 32.
[2] E. Franklin Frazier: *The Negro Church in America* (New York: Schocken Books; 1963), Chs. i–iii.

1950's had progressed to the point where Southern Negroes, together with their liberal allies, could launch an attack against segregation. The prominence of the Negro church in their struggle showed the degree to which the civil rights movement was rooted in the peculiar conditions of Negro life in the South—conditions which had made the church the central institution of the Negro subculture. Even radicals like Charles M. Sherrod of SNCC who condemned the passivity of the Negro church realized that "no one working in the South can expect to 'beat the box' if he assumes . . . that one does not need the church as it exists."[3]

The breakdown of the Southern Negro subculture in the North has recreated one of the conditions that existed under slavery, that of dangling between two cultures. Unlike other rural people who have migrated over the last hundred and forty years to the cities of the North, Southern Negroes have not been able to transplant their rural way of life even with modifications. The church decays; the family reverts to the matricentric pattern. The schools, which are segregated but at the same time controlled by white people, hold up middle-class norms to which black children are expected to conform; if they fail they are written off as "unteachable." Meanwhile the mass media flood the ghetto with images of affluence, which Negroes absorb without absorbing the ethic of disciplined self-denial and postponement of gratification that has traditionally been a central component of the materialist ethic.

In the South, the Negro church implanted an ethic of patience, suffering, and endurance. As in many peasant or precapitalist societies, this kind of religion proved surprisingly conducive—once endurance was divorced from pas-

[3] Fred Powledge: *Black Power, White Resistance: Notes on the New Civil War* (Cleveland: World Publishing Co; 1967), p. 77.

sive resignation—to effective political action. But the ethic of endurance, which is generally found among oppressed peoples in backward societies, cannot survive exposure to modern materialism. It gives way to an ethic of accumulation. Or, if real opportunities for accumulation do not exist, it gives way to hedonism, opportunism, cynicism, violence, and self-hatred—the characteristics of what Oscar Lewis calls the culture of poverty.

Lewis writes, "The culture of poverty is a relatively thin culture. . . . It does not provide much support or long-range satisfaction and its encouragement of mistrust tends to magnify helplessness and isolation. Indeed, the poverty of culture is one of the crucial aspects of the culture of poverty." These observations rest on Lewis's studies of the ghettos of Mexico City and of the Puerto Rican ghettos of San Juan and New York, where the breakdown of traditional peasant cultures has created a distinctive type of culture which comes close to being no culture at all. Something of the same thing has happened to the Negro in the North; and this helps to explain what Frazier meant when he said that the Negro's primary struggle in America had been "to acquire a culture."[4]

Some of Lewis's critics, it should be noted, argue that the concept of the culture of poverty implies a "value judgment" and a "cultural smugness" resting on ignorance of the accomplishments of this type of culture, especially of black culture. Thus Todd Gitlin, a spokesman of the New Left, advises those who write about the ghetto to "listen to Otis Redding, B. B. King, the Impressions, etc. etc." and to

---

[4] Oscar Lewis: *La Vida* (New York: Random House; 1965), p. lii. See also Oscar Lewis: *The Children of Sanchez* (New York: Random House; 1961) and *Pedro Martinez* (New York: Random House; 1964).

read Charles Keil's *Urban Blues,* which he says shows "the richness of the ghetto culture."[5]

These remarks betray a very common misunderstanding of the culture of poverty and of the concept of culture itself. Oscar Lewis is not making a "value judgment" when he says that the culture of poverty is a "thin culture." This statement has nothing in common with the cliché that Negroes are "culturally deprived"—the standard view to which Gitlin rightly objects, but which he confuses with Lewis's view. When teachers in ghetto schools say that black children are "deprived," "disadvantaged," and "unteachable," they do show a "cultural smugness" which makes them unable to talk to the children or to listen to what the children are saying. The schoolmarm's view of "culture" assumes that poems, for instance, should conform to certain rigid standards of grammar, meter, and sentiment. Thus a poem about "The Junkies," as Herbert Kohl notes, is dismissed as "the ramblings of a disturbed girl," whereas the same teacher praises "Shop with Mom" for its "pleasant and healthy thought."[6] Similarly with music: some people can't hear jazz, blues, gospel, or "soul" because it doesn't live up to their arbitrary expectations of what "good music" should sound like.

These are "value judgments" with a vengeance. But Lewis is trying to understand the culture of poverty, not in the narrow sense of the term culture but as a design for living. (Gitlin confuses the two meanings of "culture.") And what Lewis discovered in the Puerto Rican ghetto applies—urban blues notwithstanding—to the black ghetto as well: "The low aspiration level helps to reduce frustration,

[5] Todd Gitlin to editor, *New York Review of Books,* May 9, 1968, p. 40.

[6] Herbert Kohl: *Teaching the "Unteachable"* (New York: New York Review Books; 1967), pp. 11–12.

[and] the legitimization of short-range hedonism makes possible spontaneity of enjoyment," but "there is a great deal of pathos, suffering and emptiness among those who live in the culture of poverty."[7] To cite a book on the urban blues in refutation of these conclusions misses the point. The question is not whether Negro music provides a "rich" record of suffering, the question is whether the ghetto subculture gives much support to its members. It is precisely because the chief characteristics of the ghetto culture are despair and self-hatred that black nationalism has arisen as a radical cultural therapy for the ghetto.

The contrast between the comparative vitality of Negro culture in the South and the poverty of the culture of poverty explains why nationalist sects like the Nation of Islam, which have never made much headway in the South, find the Northern ghetto a fertile soil; while the civil rights movement, on the other hand, has become progressively weaker as the focus of the Negroes' struggle shifts from the South to the North.[8] The civil rights movement does not address itself to the question of how Negroes are to acquire a culture, or to the consequences of their failure to do so. It addresses itself to legal inequalities. Insofar as it implies a cultural program of any kind, the civil rights strategy proposes to integrate Negroes into the culture that already surrounds them.

Now the real objection to this is not the one so often

[7] Lewis: *La Vida*, p. lii.

[8] Both of the two leading studies of black nationalism demonstrate that nationalist movements flourish in the Northern ghetto and have little or no appeal in the rural South. See C. Eric Lincoln: *The Black Muslims in America* (Boston: Beacon Press; 1961); E. U. Essien-Udom: *Black Nationalism* (Chicago: University of Chicago Press; 1962).

given by the advocates of Black Power—that black people have nothing to gain from integrating into a culture dominated by materialistic values. Since most black people have already absorbed those values, this is a frivolous argument—especially so since it seems to imply that there is something virtuous and ennobling about poverty. What the assimilationist argument does overlook is that the civil rights movement owes its own existence, in part, to the rise of a Negro subculture in the South, and that the absence of a comparable culture in the ghetto changes the whole character of the race problem in the North. American history seems to show that a group cannot achieve "integration"—that is, equality—without first developing institutions which express and create a sense of its own distinctiveness. That is why black nationalism, which attempts to fill the cultural vacuum of the ghetto, has had a continuing attraction for Negroes, and why, even during the period of its eclipse in the thirties, forties, and fifties, nationalism won converts among the most despised and degraded elements of the Negro community in spite of the low repute in which it was held by Negro leaders.

Nationalist sects like the Black Muslims, the Black Jews, and the Moorish Temple Science movement speak to the wretchedness of the ghetto, particularly to the wretchedness of the ghetto male, in a way that the civil rights movement does not. Thus while the free and easy sexual life of the ghetto may excite the envy of outsiders, the Black Muslims correctly see it as a disrupting influence and preach a strict, "puritanical" sexual ethic. In a society in which women dominate the family and the church, the Muslims stress the role of the male as provider and protector. "Protect your women!" strikes at the heart of the humiliation of the Negro male. Similarly, the Muslims attack the hedonism of the ghetto. "Stop wasting your money!" says Elijah Muhammad. ". . . Stop spending money for tobacco, dope, cigarettes, whiskey, fine clothes, fine automobiles, expensive rugs and carpets, idleness, sport and gambling. . . . If you must have a car, buy the low-priced car."[9] Those who see in the Black Muslims no more than "the hate that hate produced" mistake the character of this movement, which joins to the mythology of racial glorification a practical program of moral rehabilitation. As one scholar has noted, the Muslim style of life is "both mystical and practical," and it is the combination of the two that "has definitely provided an escape from degradation for lower-class Negroes."[1] If anyone doubts this, he should consider the Muslims' well-documented success in redeeming, where others have failed, drug pushers, addicts, pimps, criminals of every type, the dregs of the slums. In subjecting them to a harsh, uncompromising, and admittedly authoritarian discipline, the Black Muslims and other sects have organized people who have not been organized by nonviolence, which presupposes an existing self-respect and a sense of community, or by any other form of Negro politics or religion.

[II]

Black Power represents, among other things, a revival of black nationalism and therefore cannot be regarded simply as a response to recent events. Black Power has secularized the separatist impulse which has usually (though not always) manifested itself in religious forms. Without neces-

[9] Lincoln: *The Black Muslims in America*, p. 91.
[1] Lawrence L. Tyler: "The Protestant Ethic Among the Black Muslims," *Phylon*, spring 1966, p. 11.

sarily abandoning the myth of black people as a chosen people, the new-style nationalists have secularized this myth by identifying black people in America—whom many of them continue to regard as in some sense Negroes of the diaspora—not with "the Asian Black Nation and the tribe of Shabazz," as in Black Muslim theology, but with the contemporary struggle against colonialism in the Third World. Where earlier nationalist movements, both secular and religious, envisioned physical separation from America and reunion with Islam or with Africa, many of the younger nationalists propose to fight it out here in America, by revolutionary means if necessary, and to establish— what? a black America? an America in which black people can survive as a separate "nation"? an integrated America?

Here the new-style nationalism begins to reveal underlying ambiguities which make one wonder whether it can properly be called nationalist at all. Other varieties of black nationalism—Garveyism, DuBois's Pan-Africanism, the Nation of Islam—whatever their own ambiguities, consistently sought escape from America, either to Africa, to some part of America which might be set aside for black people, or to some other part of the world. The new-style nationalists, however, view their movement as a revolution against American "colonialism" and thereby embark on a line of analysis which leads to conclusions that are not always consistent with the premise that American Negroes constitute a a "nation."

Clearly, the rhetoric of Black Power owes more to Frantz Fanon and to Che Guevara than it owes to Marcus Garvey or DuBois, let alone to Elijah Muhammad. In August 1967, Stokely Carmichael presented himself to the congress of the Organization of Latin American Solidarity in Havana as a conscious revolutionary. Claiming to speak for the black people of the United States, he is reported to have said: "We greet you as comrades because it becomes increasingly clear to us each day that we share with you a common struggle; we have a common enemy. Our enemy is white Western imperialist society; our struggle is to overthrow the system which feeds itself and expands itself through the economic and cultural exploitation of nonwhite, non-Western peoples. We speak with you, comrades, because we wish to make clear that we understand that our destinies are intertwined."[2] In a more recent speech Carmichael denies that Negroes are "black Americans" and insists that "we have *always* been an African people. . . . We got brothers in Africa, we got brothers in Cuba, we got brothers in Brazil, we got brothers in Latin America, we got brothers all over the world." Since the world is "clearly heading for a color clash," black people, Carmichael says, must arm themselves and prepare to become "the executioners of our executioners."[3]

The advocates of Black Power, it should be noted, do not have a monopoly on this type of rhetoric or on the political analysis, or lack of it, which it implies. The New Left in general more and more identifies itself with Castro, Guevara, Régis Debray, and Ho Chi Minh; many of the new radicals speak of "guerrilla warfare" against "colonialism" at home; and in fact they see the black militants, as the black militants see themselves, as the revolutionary vanguard of violent social change. The congruence of the rhetoric of Black Power with the ideology of the more demented sections of the white Left suggests that Black Power is more than a revival of Afro-American nationalism, just as

[2] John Gerassi: "Havana: A New International Is Born," unpublished MS, p. 7.

[3] Speech at Oakland Auditorium, February 17, 1968, reported in the San Francisco *Express Times,* February 22, 1968.

it is more than a response to the collapse of the civil rights movement in the North. Black Power is itself, in part, a manifestation of the New Left. It shares with the white Left not only the language of romantic anarchism but several other features as well, none of them (it must be said) conducive to its success—a pronounced distrust of people over thirty, a sense of powerlessness and despair, for which the revolutionary rhetoric serves to compensate, and a tendency to substitute rhetoric for political analysis and defiant gestures for political action. Even as they seek to disentangle themselves from the white Left, of which they are understandably contemptuous, black militants continue to share some of its worst features, the very tendencies that may indeed be destroying what strength the New Left, during its brief career, has managed to accumulate. The more these tendencies come to dominate Black Power itself, the gloomier, presumably, will be the outlook for its future.

[III]

Because Black Power has many sources, it abounds in contradictions. On the one hand Black Power derives from a tradition of Negro separatism, self-discipline, and self-help, advocating traditional "nationalist" measures ranging from cooperative businesses to proposals for complete separation. On the other hand, some of the spokesmen for Black Power contemplate guerrilla warfare against American "colonialism." In general, CORE is closer to the first position, SNCC to the second. But the ambiguity of Black Power derives from the fact that both positions frequently coexist—as in *Black Power,* the book by Stokely Carmichael and Charles V. Hamilton which was intended, apparently, to be the manifesto of the new movement but which has evoked very little enthuasism either among advocates of Black Power or among radicals in general.[4]

This book is disappointing, first of all because it makes so few concrete proposals for action, and these seem hardly revolutionary in nature: black control of black schools, black-owned businesses, and the like. Carmichael and Hamilton talk vaguely of a "major reorientation of the society" and of "the necessarily total revamping of the society" (expressions they use interchangeably) as the "central goal" of Black Power, and they urge black people not to enter coalitions with groups not similarly committed to sweeping change. But they never explain why their program demands such changes, or indeed why it would be likely to bring them about.

In order to deal with this question, one would have to discuss the relation of the ghetto to the rest of American society. To what extent does American society *depend* on the ghetto? It is undoubtedly true, as the advocates of Black Power maintain, that there is no immediate prospect that the ghettos will disappear. But it is still not clear whether the ghettos in their present state of inferiority and dependence are in some sense necessary for the functioning of American society—that is, whether powerful interests have a stake in perpetuating them—or whether they persist because American society can get along so well without black people that there is no motive either to integrate them by getting rid of the ghettos or to allow the ghettos to govern themselves. In other words, what interests have a stake in maintaining the present state of affairs? Does the welfare of

[4] Stokely Carmichael and Charles V. Hamilton: *Black Power: The Politics of Liberation in America* (New York: Random House; 1967).

General Motors depend on keeping the ghetto in a state of dependence? Would self-determination for the ghetto threaten General Motors? Carmichael and Hamilton urge black people to force white merchants out of the ghetto and to replace them with black businesses, but it is not clear why this program, aimed at businesses which themselves occupy a marginal place in American corporate capitalism, would demand or lead to a "total revamping of the society."[5]

On this point the critics of Black Power raise what appears to be a telling objection, which can be met only by clarifying the Black Power position beyond anything Carmichael and Hamilton have done. Paul Feldman writes: "A separatist black economy—unless it were to be no more than a carbon copy of the poverty that already prevails—would need black steel, black automobiles, black refrigerators. And for that, Negroes would have to take control of General Motors and US Steel: hardly an immediate prospect, and utter fantasy as long as Carmichael proposes to 'go it alone.' "[6]

But a related criticism of Black Power, that it merely proposes to substitute for white storekeepers black storekeepers who would then continue to exploit the ghetto in the same ways, seems to me to miss the point, since advocates of Black Power propose to replace white businesses with black *cooperatives*. In this respect Black Power does challenge capitalism, at least in principle; but the question remains whether a program aimed at small businessmen effectively confronts capitalism at any very sensitive point.

[5] Ibid., pp. 60–1.
[6] Paul Feldman: "The Pathos of Black Power," *Dissent,* January–February 1967, reprinted as a pamphlet by the League for Industrial Democracy, Occasional Papers, No. 8, p. 4.

Still, small businessmen, whatever their importance outside, are a sensitive issue in the ghetto and getting rid of them might do wonders for Negro morale. Not only that, but Negro cooperatives would help to reduce the flow of capital out of the ghetto, contributing thereby, if only modestly, to the accumulation of capital as well as providing employment. A "separatist black economy" is not really what Black Power seems to point to, any more than it points to exploitive Negro shopkeepers in place of white ones. "In the end," Feldman writes, "the militant-sounding proposals for a build-it-yourself black economy (a black economy, alas, without capital) remind one of . . . precisely those white moderates who preach self-help to the Negroes."[7] But Black Power envisions (or seems to envision) *collective* self-help, which is not the same thing as individualist petty capitalism on the one hand, or, on the other hand, a separate black economy.

Black Power proposes, or seems to propose, that Negroes do for themselves what other ethnic groups, faced with somewhat similar conditions, have done—advance themselves not as individuals but as groups conscious of their own special interests and identity. A comparison with other ethnic minorities in American history—the Irish, for example—is instructive. When the Irish first came to Boston, they were "the lowest of the low, lower than the Germans or Scandinavians or Jews, or even the Negroes, who had come earlier and edged a bit up the economic ladder. Irishmen were lucky if they could find part-time work on the dock or in the ditch; Irish girls hoped at best to get work as maids in hotels or in big houses on Beacon Hill. . . . The people from Ireland were a proletariat without machine

[7] Ibid.

skills or capital. Their sections of Boston were the land of the shanty Irish."[8] Excluded from all the most menial jobs ("No Irish need apply"), excluded from all social functions except their own, the Irish were also the target of vicious ethnic stereotypes. It was said that they "kept the Sabbath and everything else they could lay their hands on." "Paddy" and "Bridget" called up a definite set of images: shiftlessness, lack of ambition and work-discipline, good-natured stupidity, and incompetence. Moreover the Irish were papists and hence presumably loyal to a foreign power. Nor did they speak good English.

In the face of these disadvantages, how did the Irish escape from their shanty-town ghettos? The myth is: by individual initiative, which demonstrated ability, they overcame barriers to advancement through the usual avenues of social mobility, which eventually led to their assimilation. These commonly held assumptions about the nature of American mobility can easily be tested against a familiar case, that of the Kennedy family, which of all examples ought most nearly to fit the myth of America as a society open to individual initiative. The career of Joseph Kennedy, founder of the present dynasty, does conform in many ways to the classic entrepreneurial pattern. What is instructive about Kennedy, however, is that even by the 1920's entrepreneurial opportunities existed only on the fringes of American capitalism. By that time the normal avenue of business advancement lay in the corporate bureaucracies—and these, it is important to realize, had become increasingly the last refuge of the old American elite. As one historian has noted: "Once it became clear that political control of the

---

[8] James MacGregor Burns: *John Kennedy: A Political Profile* (New York: Harcourt, Brace; 1959), p. 6.

big cities would inevitably pass into the hands of the immigrant groups, Big Business came to be regarded as a new preserve of the older Americans, where their status and influence could continue to flourish."[9] The result was that "the social patterns established within Big Business bureaucracies at the turn of the century helped to close off key areas of the economy and to keep them virtually impenetrable to even the most gifted outsiders. For one without the background, etiquette, and personal appearance to 'fit in,' and without sponsors to smooth his way, a career in one of the major corporations would be more like scaling a high wall than climbing a ladder."[1] The corporate bureaucracies readily adapted themselves to the purposes of ethnic exclusiveness because success in the bureaucratic career, by its very nature, depends on the accumulation of educational advantages, on family connections, and on other signs of social status. A study of 185 business leaders between 1901 and 1910 shows that while fourteen per cent had either founded or bought the business in which they now occupied the top positions, twenty-seven per cent inherited their positions, while all the rest "climbed the bureaucratic ladder, not infrequently, of course, after their family status, education, and other social endowments helped them get the proper start."[2]

Endowed with several advantages at the start of his career, notably a Harvard degree and marriage into the powerful Fitzgerald family, Joseph Kennedy was president of a

[9] Moses Rischin: *The American Gospel of Success* (Chicago: Quadrangle Books; 1965), p. 9.

[1] Ibid., p. 10.

[2] William Miller: "The Business Elite in Business Bureaucracies," in William Miller, ed.: *Men in Business* (Cambridge: Harvard University Press; 1952), p. 290.

small bank in Boston by the time he was twenty-five. "But many a Yankee banker still could not wholly accept Joe Kennedy. It was all right for Irishmen to run little East Boston banks and handle immigrants' remittances, they felt, but not to crash the central citadels of finance. So Kennedy, disgusted, began to operate more and more in New York and Hollywood."[3] His successful speculations on the West Coast, followed by even more spectacular operations on Wall Street in the early twenties, testified to Kennedy's financial genius but also to the degree to which the normal bureaucratic career was closed off to ethnic minorities. It is highly misleading to think that in American history those minorities have escaped poverty through the dominant institutions of the surrounding culture. On the contrary, they have succeeded in marginal institutions, a fact that incidentally reveals one dimension of the present race problem—the decline of entrepreneurial capitalism in a mature industrial economy.[4]

Entrepreneurial opportunities, however, are only part of the story, even in the case of earlier minorities. Those opportunities could not have been exploited if groups like the Irish had not already achieved a strong sense of ethnic solidarity. In the case of the Kennedy family, it is important to note that Joseph Kennedy's career rested solidly on the achievements of the previous generation. Both his own fa-

---

[3] Burns: *John Kennedy,* p. 16.

[4] A more important consequence of technological maturity, of course, is the growing obsolescence of unskilled and semiskilled labor. See *Report of the National Advisory Commission on Civil Disorders* (New York: E. P. Dutton; 1968), p. 278; also Carmichael: speech in Oakland (San Francisco *Express Times,* February 22, 1968): "This country is becoming more and more technological so that the need for black people is fastly disappearing."

ther, Patrick J. Kennedy, and his father-in-law, John F. Fitzgerald, had already "advanced far up into the ranks of middle-class respectability" by selling things to other Irishmen (liquor, for instance) and by capturing their votes, "thus stor[ing] up influence to trade in the political arena."[5] Both saloon-keeping and machine politics represented a form of collective self-help in the Irish ghetto; they depended on a sense of Irish solidarity. In effect, the Irish created their own institutions parallel to the official institutions of American society: the saloon, the Irish-American church, above all the political machine. "Unable to participate in the normal associational affairs of the community," Oscar Handlin writes, "the Irish felt obliged to erect a society within a society, to act together in their own way. In every contact therefore the group . . . became intensely aware of its peculiar and exclusive identity."[6] The Irish did not advance as individuals, they advanced as a group, drastically altering the structure of urban politics in the process. Nor did they lose their ethnic character through assimilation into American life; politicians recognize this when they cater to the "Irish vote." As Harold Cruse observes, "Every four years the great fiction of the assimilated American (white and/or Protestant) ideal is put aside to deal with the pluralistic reality of the hyphenated-American vote."[7] The rest of the time this reality is swallowed up in the rhetoric of opportunity and individualism.

The assertion that "the individual in America has few

[5] Burns, *John Kennedy*, p. 8.

[6] Oscar Handlin: *Boston's Immigrants* (rev. edn., Cambridge: Harvard University Press; 1959), p. 176.

[7] Cruse: *The Crisis of the Negro Intellectual*, p. 6. The true character of American society, according to Cruse, is that of a botched pluralism—"a badly bungled process of inter-group cultural fusion." (Ibid., p. 456.)

rights that are not backed up by the political, economic and social power of one group or another"[8] is borne out not only in the case of the Irish but even more clearly in the case of the Jews. Like the Irish, the Jews escaped extreme poverty through the labor movement or through marginal businesses or professions serving a largely Jewish clientele. To a degree that is seldom recognized, Jewish life in America is self-contained. According to a recent study of Jews in a midwestern city, the Jews after three generations still live in "separate but equal" communities "that endure in spite of all sociological predictions to the contrary."[9] Even Jews who have achieved wealth and status in the Jewish community, recognizing that they lack the qualifications for membership in the upper class of the gentile world (family status, social connections, and high-status occupations), are "understandably reluctant to sever their remaining ties with the Jewish community. The community, and their special relation to it, is, after all, the precondition of their status."[1]

In spite of the decline of overt anti-Semitism, the Jews in this city (Minneapolis?) and elsewhere—except for those in the intellectual community, which is exempt from these generalizations—still live in their own separate and self-sufficient community. They derive important advantages from separation of which Jewish businessmen, for example, are well aware.

"In a period of growing oligopoly, Jewish businesses have survived in the shelter of ethnic segregation. Because Jews are excluded from the dominant business community,

---

[8] Ibid., p. 8.

[9] Judith R. Kramer and Seymour Levantman: *Children of the Gilded Ghetto: Conflict Resolutions of Three Generations of American Jews* (New Haven: Yale University Press; 1961), p. xi.

[1] Ibid., pp. 117–18.

they are beyond the reach of its informal sanctions. They are 'outsiders,' marginal retail traders, who have no reason to be susceptible to the opinion of gentile colleagues who do not accept them in any case."

Thus Jewish businessmen continue to prefer a flexible price system to fixed prices, thereby performing "considerable economic service as middlemen for inflation-conscious consumers and overstocked manufacturers, at the cost, however, of their social honor in the larger business community."[2] Similarly Jewish doctors serve Jewish patients, Jewish lawyers predominantly Jewish clients. "Exploiting their marginality for their own advantage has been the one means of economic survival consistently available to Jews."[3] One of the marginal opportunities open to Jewish entrepreneurs, it should be added, is the black ghetto. Thus in spite of their services to the civil rights movement, Jews now find themselves singled out as special objects of the wrath of black militants. "It is now widely accepted as an incontrovertible fact that . . . there exists a pronounced anti-Jewish sentiment among the Negro masses in this country."[4]

The history of American ethnic-group pluralism does not support the integrationist assumption that individual initiative has been the traditional mechanism of social mobility. Those who urge Negroes to advance themselves through the "regular" channels of personal mobility ignore the experience of earlier minorities, the relevance of which is obscured both by the tendency to view the history of immigration as a triumph of assimilation and by the individualist

[2] Ibid., p. 2.
[3] Ibid., pp. 68–9.
[4] Shlomo Katz, ed.: *Negro and Jew* (New York: Macmillan; 1967), p. vii.

premises which persistently blind Americans to the importance of collective phenomena and therefore to most of history.[5]

[IV]

The history of other minorities in the United States supports the contention of Black Power theorists that group solidarity is an essential precondition of power. Nevertheless the advocates of Black Power seem reluctant to draw the full implications from this parallel or to explore its theoretical limits. Carmichael and Hamilton, for instance, men-

---

[5] "A preponderant number of the [Italian] immigrants made sacrifices of present consumption to capitalize their children. The effort had no support from liberals nor an anti-poverty program. The Italians who succeeded built on their Italian qualities. They individuated successfully not by trying to bury themselves in the Anglo-Saxon mass, but by capitalizing on their own individualism. This is the fundamental lesson for the Negro." (J. A. Raffaele to editor, *New York Review of Books,* May 9, 1968, p. 41.)

This statement is a perfect example of the myth of individualism. Black people have, of course, been trying for a long time to do just what Professor Raffaele urges them to do; but the apparent futility of their individual efforts suggests the need to re-examine the whole history of ethnic groups in America. Recent studies do not seem to bear out his assertion that "immigrants made sacrifices of present consumption to capitalize their children." One of the interesting conclusions to emerge from Stefan Thernstrom's study of Irish workers in Newburyport, Massachusetts (*Poverty and Progress: Social Mobility in a Nineteenth Century City* [Cambridge: Harvard University Press; 1964], p. 177) is that the Irish often achieved "property mobility" at the *expense* of their children, or at least at the expense of "the forms of mobility which required education." Since there are not yet any comparably thorough studies of Italian immigrants, it would be foolish to dismiss out of hand the possibility that similar patterns of mobility may be discovered in their history, or the more general possibility that we have been led badly astray, all along the line, by the myth of American individualism.

tion the parallel with other ethnic groups, but only in passing, and without noticing that this analogy undermines the analogy with colonial people which they draw elsewhere in their manifesto, wherever their militant rhetoric appears to demand it. They observe, correctly, that on the evidence of ethnic voting "the American pot has not melted," politically at least, and they recognize that "traditionally, each new ethnic group in this society has found the route to social and political viability through the organization of its own institutions." But they do not explain how this analysis of the Negroes' situation squares with the argument that "black people in this country form a colony and it is not in the interest of the colonial power to liberate them."[6]

Quite apart from this inconsistency, the ethnic parallel, whether or not it finally proves useful, needs to be systematically explored. Did the struggles of other minorities contribute to a "major reorientation of the society"? Not if a "major reorientation" is equivalent to the "complete revision" of American institutions, which is the precondition, according to Carmichael and Hamilton, of black liberation.[7] Perhaps the analogy is therefore misleading and should be abandoned. On the other hand, it may be that the special institutions created by other nationalities in America—like the political machine and crime syndicates, to name only two examples—do in fact represent "major reorientations," even though they fall somewhat short of a "total revamping" or "complete revision" of society. These institutions were defined as illegitimate and resisted by the rest of society, but they were finally absorbed after protracted struggles, as a result of which American society was

---

[6] Carmichael and Hamilton: *Black Power,* pp. 44–5, 5.
[7] Ibid., p. 66.

changed in important ways. Perhaps it is confusing, then, to think of "major reorientations" as synonymous with "complete revisions," particularly when the nature of the changes proposed remains so indeterminate. In that case it is the colonial analogy that should be dropped, as contributing to the confusion.

Black Power contains many other examples of sloppy analysis and the failure to pursue any line of reasoning through to its consequences. Basic questions are left in doubt. Is the Negro issue a class issue, a race issue, or a "national" (ethnic) issue? Treating it as a class issue—as the authors appear to do when they write that the "only coalition which seems acceptable to us," in the long run, is "a coalition of poor blacks and poor whites"—further weakens the ethnic analogy and blurs the concept of black people as a "nation"—the essential premise, one would think, of "Black Power."[8]

Paul Feldman seems to me on the wrong track when he accuses SNCC of resorting to "what is primarily a racial rather than an economic approach."[9] On the contrary, the advocates of Black Power tend, if anything, toward a misplaced class analysis, derived from popularized Marxism or from Castroism, which considers the American Negro as an exploited proletarian. Thus Carmichael and Hamilton try to sustain their analogy of the Negroes as a "colonial" people by arguing that the Negro communities "export" cheap labor.[1] This may be true of the South, where Negroes do represent cheap labor (although mechanization is changing the situation even in the South) and where racism, accord-

[8] Ibid., p. 82.
[9] Feldman: *The Pathos of Black Power,* p. 9.
[1] Carmichael and Hamilton: *Black Power,* p. 6.

ingly, is functionally necessary as a way of maintaining class exploitation. Here the Negroes might be mobilized behind a program of class action designed to change society in fundamental ways.[2] In the North, however, the essential feature of the Negro's situation is precisely his dispensability, which is increasingly evident in the growing unemployment of Negro men, particularly young men. As Bayard Rustin has pointed out, ghetto Negroes do not constitute an exploited proletariat. They should be regarded not as a working class but as a lower class or *lumpenproletariat*. "The distinction," he writes, "is important. The working class is employed. It has a relation to the production of goods and services; much of it is organized in unions. It enjoys a measure of cohesion, discipline and stability lacking in the lower class. The latter is unemployed or marginally employed. It is relatively unorganized, incohesive, unstable. It contains the petty criminal and antisocial elements. Above all, unlike the working class, it lacks the sense of a stake in society. When the slum proletariat is black, its alienation is even greater."[3]

It is precisely these conditions, however, that make Black Power more relevant to the ghetto than "civil rights," if

[2] This does not mean, however, that Southern Negroes will be receptive to the rhetoric of alienation, which depicts Negroes as a revolutionary vanguard. On the contrary, the Northern radicals at the Conference for New Politics failed to stir the delegates from the Mississippi Freedom Democratic party with their "easy talk about violence and guerrilla warfare," as Feldman notes in an unpublished report on the conference. The rhetoric of alienation addresses itself not to the actual class situation of the Southern Negro sharecropper or tenant but to the rootlessness and despair of the Northern Negro. (Paul Feldman: "Report to the LID Board of Directors on the New Politics Convention," unpublished MS, September 30, 1967, p. 14.)

[3] Bayard Rustin: *Which Way Out?* (League for Industrial Democracy, Occasional Papers, No. 9), p. 4.

Black Power is understood as a form of ethnic solidarity which addresses itself to the instability and to the "antisocial" elements of ghetto life, and tries to organize and "socialize" those elements around a program of collective self-help. The potential usefulness of black nationalism, in other words, lies in its ability to organize groups which neither the church, the unions, the political parties, nor the social workers have been able to organize. Rustin's analysis, while it effectively refutes the idea that the Negro lower class can become a revolutionary political force in any conventional sense, does not necessarily lead one to reject Black Power altogether, as he does, or to endorse "coalitions." Actually it can be used as an argument *against* coalitions, on the grounds that a marginal lower class has no interests in common with, say, the labor movement. If the Negroes are a lower class as opposed to a working class, it is hard to see, theoretically, why the labor movement is "foremost among [the Negroes'] political allies," as Paul Feldman believes.[4] Theory aside, experience does not bear out this contention.

Concerning the revolutionary potential of Black Power, however, Rustin seems to me absolutely right. "From the revolutionist point of view," he says, "the question is not whether steps could be taken to strengthen organization among the *lumpenproletariat* but whether that group could be a central agent of social transformation. Generally, the answer has been no."[5] But these observations, again, do not necessarily lead to the conclusion that Black Power has no validity. Rather they suggest the need to divorce Black Power as a program of collective self-advancement from the revolutionary rhetoric of the New Left, while at the same

[4] Feldman: *The Pathos of Black Power,* p. 8.
[5] Rustin: *Which Way Out?* p. 4.

time they remind us that other ethnic minorities, faced with somewhat similar conditions, created new institutions that had important (though not revolutionary) social consequences. Black people cannot be considered a "nation" and a revolutionary *class* at the same time.

[V]

Nathan Wright's *Black Power and Urban Unrest,* another attempt to define the meaning of Black Power, shares with the Carmichael-Hamilton book a tendency to ignore important theoretical questions or to discuss them without sufficient awareness of their implications. Nevertheless, the two books seem to have quite different conceptions of Black Power. As chairman of the Newark conference on Black Power last July, Dr. Wright, an Episcopal clergyman, appeared in the public eye as a militant. But Black Power seems to mean to him little more than the control by Negroes of civil rights organizations like SNCC and CORE (of which he is a long-time member). He does not appear to quarrel with the previous *aims* of those organizations. That is, he does not advocate black separatism, but "desegregation," which he insists should be distinguished from integration.[6] Integration, Wright argues, has come to imply assimilation, which undermines Negro self-respect, thwarts the black man's struggle for "responsible selfhood," and perpetuates his dependence on whites. "Desegregation," on the other hand—"the universal goal," according to Wright, of "all other rising ethnic groups" in America—means that Negroes should have access to the same facilities and the

[6] Nathan Wright, Jr.: *Black Power and Urban Unrest* (New York: Hawthorne Books; 1967), p. 45.

same opportunities as everyone else, without forfeiting their identity as Negroes.[7]

As an abstract proposition, this distinction is reasonably clear, but it is hard to see how it applies to concrete issues like housing and schools. How can "desegregation" in housing be distinguished from "integration"? If "desegregated" housing means anything, it means the disappearance of ethnic neighborhoods (something, incidentally, which has not yet happened in the case of other minorities) and the assimilation of Negroes into white neighborhoods. Similarly, the schools are in any case already "desegregated," in the sense that they try to inculcate black children with white norms and judge them by white standards of achievement.[8]

Some people, Dr. Wright among them, propose to solve this problem by getting more Negroes on school boards. At one point Wright urges Negroes to band together "to seek executive positions in corporations, bishoprics, deanships of cathedrals, superintendencies of schools, and high-management positions in banks, stores, investment houses, legal firms, civic and government agencies, and factories."[9] This is, of course, exactly what many Negroes are doing already, but there is little reason to think that the trickle of middle-class Negroes into executive positions, where they are used as window dressing, will lead to "a radically new power balance," as Dr. Wright insists.[1] Like Carmichael and Hamilton, he occasionally makes a parallel between Negroes and other ethnic groups, but he does not draw the

[7] Ibid., pp. 20, 131.

[8] On ghetto schools see Herbert Kohl: *Teaching the "Unteachable,"* and his *36 children* (New York: New American Library; 1967); also Jonathan Kozol: *Death at an Early Age* (Boston: Houghton Mifflin; 1967).

[9] Wright: *Black Power and Urban Unrest,* p. 43.

[1] Ibid.

proper conclusion from their history. Other ethnic groups achieved a larger share of power not by penetrating established institutions but by improvising their own institutions, which gave them political, economic, and cultural leverage as groups. They could not have achieved this leverage as upwardly mobile individuals. Irish Catholics did not win power by getting to be heads of corporations, infiltrating the Republican party, or becoming respectable leaders of municipal reform; they won power by creating the urban political machine.

Dr. Wright further confuses matters by criticizing Negro leaders for not advocating "social equality." He remarks that "no major civil rights leader, even today, espouses as a major plank in his platform social equality, at the very heart of which is the matter of intermarriage. Yet economic survival and advancement, as well as a sense of pride, depend in no small degree upon relationships of a blood and legal variety."[2] These observations seem to me to reveal a misunderstanding of the way in which intermarriage, historically, always tends to erode a sense of ethnic allegiance—which is why it has always been opposed by those wishing to preserve a sense of nationality, including most advocates of Black Power. Nor is the rate of intermarriage a reliable indication of a group's attainment of power, as Dr. Wright's remarks seem to imply. Intermarriage represents the intellectual's longed-for emancipation from what he regards as narrow ethnic prejudices, but the cultural emancipation of intellectuals, which often turns out to be illusory anyway, has nothing to do with the distribution of power in society. As an important social goal, intermarriage is utterly irrelevant.

[2] Ibid., p. 16.

[VI]

By repudiating their white supporters, the advocates of Black Power have sent a moral shock through the liberal community, which two white veterans of the civil rights movement in different ways record. Charles E. Fager, a Northern radical and the younger of the two, has adjusted to the trauma of Black Power, and now defends it not only as an appropriate strategy for black people but as a strategy which makes clearer than before the kind of measures white radicals should take toward reorganizing their own communities. Fred Powledge, a Southerner and free-lance journalist who was formerly a reporter for *The New York Times,* sympathetically observed the civil rights movement in the South first hand. He deplores the rise of black separatism, which he is convinced "will not work."[3]

By separatism Powledge means "the construction of parallel societies, black and white." This is "impossible," he thinks, because "black institutions, built alongside existing white ones, would be poverty-stricken by comparison." Moreover, separatist "demagogues" would have to use violence "as an organizing tool" in order to keep the black community in line; and if that happened, "the white majority would respond with near-genocide."[4] Integration, on the other hand, does not necessarily mean assimilation. In fact Powledge thinks that it is "essential" for the civil rights movement to "stamp out the idea, held so long by so many white liberals who did not even know that they held it, that integration consists of turning *'them'* white."[5]

---

[3] Powledge: *Black Power, White Resistance,* p. 261.
[4] Ibid., pp. 261, 264.
[5] Ibid., p. 265.

Powledge's position resembles Nathan Wright's. Both writers advocate integration or desegregation—that is, equal rights and equal opportunities—while opposing assimilation on the one hand and black separatism on the other. If Black Power means that Negroes should not straighten their hair in order to win illusory acceptance by whites, then both Powledge and Wright support it. Nor does Powledge deny that, within the civil rights movement, Negroes should "run the show."[6] When he urges whites to restrict themselves to contributing their special skills to a movement led largely by Negroes, he agrees not only with Wright, but with Carmichael and Hamilton, who believe that white people are most effective in "supportive" roles.[7] Since neither Wright nor Carmichael and Hamilton advocate the conception of black separatism which Powledge attacks, one begins to wonder whether the whole controversy about Black Power doesn't boil down to a dispute about certain words. Everybody, it seems, supports Black Power and, at the same time, favors "integration."

But as Stokely Carmichael has pointed out, "You can *integrate communities,* but you *assimilate individuals.*"[8] Until black people become a community, in Carmichael's view, efforts to integrate them necessarily imply assimilation. Here is the irreducible difference between the integrationist and Black Power positions. Fager's book helps to clarify the debate. Without indulging in the liberal-baiting that so often accompanies discussions of Black Power, he challenges integrationists to demonstrate why "integration" does not work out in practice to mean assimilation, whereby a few middle-class Negroes are provisionally admitted to white

[6] Ibid., p. 266.
[7] Carmichael and Hamilton: *Black Power,* p. 83.
[8] Quoted in Fager: *White Reflections on Black Power,* p. 27.

society, leaving the others behind in the ghetto as unassimilable. According to Fager, this is certainly the way things have worked out so far. If more money were spent on education and welfare programs, he argues, the rate of mobility could be speeded up, but it is unlikely that the ghettos could be completely eradicated—not for a long time, anyway, and in the meantime more assimilation at the top will merely add to the hatreds and frustrations at the bottom of Negro society.[9]

Whereas Bayard Rustin and others argue that Negroes cannot hope to win equality except in coalition with other groups, Fager believes, as do other advocates of Black Power, that at the present time the black community is not cohesive enough to enter into coalitions without being swallowed up. As a white radical who until recently worked in the civil rights coalition, he is left with the question of where next to turn his energies. He tries to show that Black Power demands of white liberals a parallel strategy, based on the premise that the "liberal community," like the Negro community, "does not control the institutions around and through which its life is organized and controlled." Each of these communities must therefore develop "an economic base which it can control, which can support the community substantially, and which can confront other power groups as equals." Young radicals should "go back to school" and acquire the skills necessary to run parallel and

---

[9] Bayard Rustin himself writes that "the day-to-day lot of the ghetto Negro has not been improved by the various judicial and legislative measures of the past decade." Under these circumstances, "the belief that the ghetto is destined to last forever," which Rustin sees as the major premise of Black Power, makes a good deal of sense. (Rustin: "Black Power and Coalition Politics," *Commentary,* September 1966, pp. 37–8.) The ghetto is more likely to last for a long time than to be eradicated in the near future.

competing institutions which will free the "liberal community" from its dependence on established structures, while the older radicals should "figure out how to withdraw their money and abilities as much as possible from status quo institutions and rechannel the *bulk* of them into the development and support of independent-base institutions."[1]

Unfortunately these suggestions are exceedingly vague, although they are not much more vague than the strategy of Black Power itself. Fager's effort to translate Black Power into its white equivalent unintentionally reveals the poverty of Black Power as a political strategy. For while a program of collective self-help seems closer than civil rights solutions to the psychological and even to the economic needs of the ghetto, the advocates of Black Power have not been able to explain what such a program means in practice or what kind of strategy would be necessary to achieve it. This is probably why they spend so much time talking not about politics but about therapy. By detaching Black Power from its context—the psychic and spiritual malaise of the ghetto, which Black Power, like other versions of black nationalism, is designed to cure—Fager makes clear what we had already begun to suspect, that Black Power not only contains no political ideas that are applicable elsewhere, it contains very few political ideas at all. As a program of spiritual regeneration, it offers hope to people whom the civil rights movement ignores or does not touch; though, even here, Black Power may prove to be less successful than the religious versions of black nationalism, since it can appeal neither to the mystic brotherhood nor to the authoritarian discipline of the Black Muslims. As a political program, Black Power does not explain how Negro cooperatives are

[1] Fager: *White Reflections on Black Power,* pp. 94, 99.

to come into being or what they will use for money, how the ghettos are to control and pay for their own schools, or why, even if these programs were successful, they would lead to sweeping changes in American society as a whole.

Are the proponents of Black Power capable of formulating a workable strategy? Are they even interested in formulating a strategy? Although Black Power does address itself to certain problems of the ghetto which other approaches ignore, one cannot even say with confidence that the emergence of Black Power is a hopeful sign, which, if nothing else, will teach black people to stop hating their own blackness. If it merely teaches them to hate whiteness instead, it will contribute to the nihilistic emotions building up in the ghetto, and thus help to bring about the race war which spokesmen for Black Power, until recently at least, claimed they were trying to prevent. Insofar as Black Power represents an effort to discipline the anger of the ghettos and to direct this anger toward radical action, it works against the resentment and despair of the ghetto, which may nevertheless overwhelm it. But Black Power is not only an attack on this despair, it is also, in part, its product, and reflects forces which it cannot control.

In the last few months, we have seen more and more vivid examples of the way in which Black Power has come to be associated with mindless violence—as in the disturbances at San Francisco State College in the fall of 1967—and with a "revolutionary" rhetoric that conceals a growing uncertainty of purpose.[2] It becomes increasingly clear that many of the intellectuals who talk of Black Power do not understand the difference between riots and revolution, and

[2] On San Francisco State see "Chaos on the Campus," *New Republic,* January 6, 1968, pp. 14–15.

that they have no program capable of controlling the growing violence of the ghetto. It is also becoming clear that in fact they have not only given up the effort to control violence or even to understand it, but are themselves making a cult of violence, and by doing so are abdicating leadership of their own movement. Meanwhile white radicals, who supposedly know better but are just as foolish and patronizing about Black Power as they were about civil rights, applaud from the sidelines or, as at San Francisco State, join the destruction, without perceiving that it is radicalism itself that is being destroyed.

[VII]

The nihilistic tendencies latent in Black Power have been identified and analyzed not only by the advocates of "liberal" coalitions. The most penetrating study of these tendencies is to be found in Harold Cruse's *The Crisis of the Negro Intellectual,* which is also a critique of integration and a defense of black nationalism. Cruse is a radical, but his book gives no comfort to the "radicalism" currently fashionable. It deals with real issues, not leftist fantasies. Cruse understands that radicals need clarity more than they need revolutionary purity, and he refuses to be taken in by loud exclamations of militancy which conceal an essential flabbiness of purpose. At a time when Negro intellectuals are expected to show their devotion to the cause by acting out a ritual and expiatory return to the dress and manners of their "people"—when intellectuals of all nationalities are held to be the very symbol of futility, and when even a respected journalist like Andrew Kopkind can write that "the responsibility of the intellectual is the same as that of the street organizer, the draft resister, the Digger: to talk *to* people, not *about* them"—Cruse feels no need to apologize for the intellectual's work, which is to clarify issues.[3] It is because Negro intellectuals have almost uniformly failed in this work that he judges them, at his angriest and most impatient, a "colossal fraud"—a judgment that applies without much modification to white intellectuals, now as in the recent past.[4]

The Crisis of the Negro Intellectual is a history of the Negro Left since the First World War. When all the manifestoes and polemics of the sixties are forgotten, this book will survive as a monument of historical analysis—a notable contribution to the understanding of the American past, but more than that, a vindication of historical analysis as the best way, maybe the only way, of gaining a clear understanding of social issues.

As a historian, an intellectual, a Negro, and, above all perhaps, as a man who came of political age in the 1940's, Cruse sees more clearly than the young black nationalists of the sixties how easily Negro radicals—integrationists and nationalists alike—become "disoriented prisoners of white leftists, no matter how militant they sound."[5] Instead of devising strategies appropriate to the special situation of American Negroes, they import ideologies which have no relevance to that situation and which subordinate the needs of American Negroes to an abstract model of revolutionary change. Marxism is such a model, and a considerable portion of Cruse's book elaborates and documents the thesis that American Marxism has disastrously misled Negro intellectuals over a period of fifty years.

---

[3] Andrew Kopkind: "Soul Power," *New York Review of Books,* August 24, 1967, p. 3.
[4] Cruse: *The Crisis of the Negro Intellectual,* p. 373.
[5] Ibid., p. 416.

But the ideology of guerrilla warfare, which in some Black Power circles has replaced Marxism as the current mode, equally ignores American realities. According to Cruse, "The black ghettoes are in dire need of new organizations or parties of a political nature, yet it is a fact that most of the leading young nationalist spokesmen are apolitical. . . . The black ghettoes are in even more dire need of every possible kind of economic and self-help organization, and a buyers and consumers council, but the most militant young nationalists openly ridicule such efforts as reformist and a waste of time. For them politics and economics are most unrevolutionary. What they do consider revolutionary are Watts-type uprisings—which lead nowhere."[6]

Black Power—with or without the guerrilla rhetoric—is a "strategic retreat." "It proposes to change, not the white world outside, but the black world inside, by reforming it into something else politically or economically." The Muslims, Cruse points out, have "already achieved this in a limited way, substituting religion for politics"; and Malcolm X (whom the advocates of Black Power now list as one of their patron saints) quit the Black Muslims precisely because "this type of Black Power lacked a dynamic, was static and aloof to the broad struggle." By emphasizing "Psychological Warfare" as "Phase I" of Black Power, as one of the new nationalists puts it, the advocates of Black Power have placed themselves "almost in the lap of the Nation of Islam."[7] Moreover, they have reversed the proper order of priorities, according to Cruse, for "psychological equality" must be the product, not the precondition, of cultural regeneration and political power.

[6] Ibid., p. 441.
[7] Ibid., p. 548.

He thinks that integrationists, on the other hand, while they may have addressed themselves to the "broad struggle," conceive of the struggle in the wrong terms. They waste their strength fighting prejudice, when they ought to be organizing the ghetto so that it could exert more influence, say, over the use of antipoverty funds. Instead of trying to change the Constitution in order to make it "reflect the social reality of America as a nation of nations, or a nation of ethnic groups," even advocates of violence like Robert Williams propose merely to "implement" the Constitution, with, in Williams's words, "justice and equality for all people."[8] Cruse accuses integrationists of being taken in by the dominant mythology of American individualism and of failing to see the importance of collective action along ethnic lines, or—even worse—of mistakenly conceiving collective action in class terms which are irrelevant to the Negro's situation in America.

Cruse himself is a Marxist—that is, a historical materialist. But he opposes the obstinate effort to impose on the Negro problem a class analysis which sees Negroes as an oppressed proletariat. He thinks this obscures, among other things, the nature of the Negro middle class and the role it plays in American life. Actually "middle class" is a misnomer, because this class is not a real bourgeoisie. The most important thing about it is that "Negro businessmen must depend on the Negro group for their support," which according to Cruse means two things: Negro businessmen are more closely tied to the Negro nation than to their white middle-class counterparts, no matter how hard they may struggle against this identification; and they occupy a marginal position in American capitalism as a whole, since

[8] Ibid., pp. 393–4.

black capitalism can only function in limited areas—personal services to the Negro community, such as barbershops, insurance companies, etc.—which white capitalism does not choose to enter.[9]

Because of its marginal position, the black bourgeoisie does not have the resources to support Negro institutions —a theater, for instance—which might help to give the Negro community some consciousness of itself. Negro intellectuals thus depend on white intellectuals—or white foundations—as much as Negro maids depend on white housewives, even though the intellectual world, according to Cruse, is the only realm in which genuine integration has taken place or is likely to take place. Even there, Negroes have been forced to compete at a disadvantage. They have had to regard their white counterparts not only as colleagues but as patrons. Hence the dominance of Jews in the Negro-Jewish coalition that has been characteristic of American Marxist movement.

The effort to explain how this coalition emerged and what it did to Negro radicalism occupies the better part of *The Crisis of the Negro Intellectual*. The history of the Negro intellectual from the 1920's to the present necessarily becomes a history of American Marxism as well. Cruse begins with the "Harlem renaissance," when Marcus Garvey's version of black nationalism was only one of many signs of cultural and political awakening among American Negroes, and he shows, step by step, how Negro intellectuals retreated from these promising beginnings and began to preach culturally sterile and politically futile doctrines of proletarian uplift. Thus in the twenties and thirties Negro intellectuals lent themselves to the communists' efforts to

[9] Ibid., p. 174.

convince Moscow that American Negroes could become the spearhead of a proletarian revolution. A delegation of Negro communists in Moscow claimed in 1922 that "in five years we will have the American revolution"—just as Stokely Carmichael now carries a similar message to Havana. "I listened to the American delegates deliberately telling lies about conditions in America," wrote Claude McKay, "and I was disgusted."[1]

Thirty-eight years later Harold Cruse found himself in a somewhat similar position in Castro's Cuba, where he had gone with LeRoi Jones and other Americans "to 'see for ourselves' what it was all about." "The ideology of a new revolutionary wave in the world at large had lifted us out of the anonymity of the lonely struggle in the United States to the glorified rank of visiting dignitaries. . . . Nothing in our American experience had ever been as arduous and exhausting as this journey. Our reward was the prize of revolutionary protocol that favored those victims of capitalism away from home." But in the midst of this "ideological enchantment," none of the delegates bothered to ask: *"What did it all mean and how did it relate to the Negro in America?"*[2]

The new-wave Negro miltants, like their forerunners of the 1930's, "have taken on a radical veneer without radical substance" and have formulated "no comprehensive radical philosophy to replace either the liberalism they denounce or the radicalism of the past that bred them."[3] In a chapter on "The Intellectuals and Force and Violence"—in some ways the most important chapter in the book—Cruse examines a

[1] Ibid., p. 55.
[2] Ibid., p. 357.
[3] Ibid., p. 202.

notable instance of the prevailing confusion among Negro radicals (shared by white radicals): the cult of "armed self-defense" as a form of revolutionary action. Robert Williams, an officer of the NAACP, raised the issue of self-defense in Monroe, North Carolina, in 1959, when he armed his followers against the Ku Klux Klan. In the uproar following the NAACP's suspension of Williams and his deification by the new black Left, basic questions went unanswered. For one thing, violence in the South, where it is directed against the Klan, has been strategically different from violence in the North, where it has been directed against the National Guard. For another, the issue of armed self-defense does not touch the deep-rooted conditions that have to be changed if the Negro's position is to be changed. Violence, Cruse argues, becomes a meaningful strategy only insofar as American institutions resist radical change and resist it violently. Since the Negro movement has not yet even formulated a program for radical change, violence is tactically premature; and, in any case, "the *main* front of tactics must always be organizational and institutional."[4]

Neither the black Left nor the white Left, however, understands that an American revolution (even if it were imminent, which it isn't) "would have very little in common with the foreign revolutions they have read about."[5] Lacking a theory, lacking any understanding of history, confusing violent protest with radicalism, black radicals persist in yet another mistake—the equation of pro-blackness with hatred of whites. Violent hatred fills the vacuum left by the lack of an ideology and a program. Long before the new radicals came on the scene, Cruse writes, "this had been

[4] Ibid., p. 360.
[5] Ibid., p. 371.

one of the Negro intellectual's most severe 'hang-ups' "—
one that in our own time threatens to become the driving
force of the Negro movement. "This situation results from a
psychology that is rooted in the Negro's symbiotic 'blood-
ties' to the white Anglo-Saxon. It is the culmination of that
racial drama of love and hate between slave and master,
bound together in the purgatory of plantations." The self-
advancement of the Negro community, however, cannot
rest on ambivalent hatreds. "All race hate is self-defeating
in the long run because it distorts the critical faculties."[6]

[VIII]

The Crisis of the Negro Intellectual—the complexity and
richness of which is difficult to convey in a summary—
documents not only the failure of Negro radicalism but the
failure of American radicalism in general, which lives off
imported ideologies and myths of imminent revolution in
which Negroes have always been assigned a leading part.
Reading this book today, in the wake of such disasters as
the Conference for New Politics, one realizes how little has
changed, and how, in spite of its determination to avoid the
mistakes of the radicals of the thirties and forties, the New
Left remains trapped in the rhetoric and postures of its
predecessors. The Left today should be concerned not only
with the long-range problem of creating new institutions of
popular democracy (a subject to which it has given very
little thought) but with the immediate problem of saving
what remains of liberalism—free speech, safeguards against
arbitrary authority, separation of powers—without which

---

[6] Ibid., pp. 363–5.

further democratic experiments of any kind will come to an end.

The Left should take seriously the possibility which it rhetorically proclaims—that the crisis of American colonialism abroad, together with the failure of welfare programs to improve conditions in the ghetto, will generate a demand for thoroughgoing repression which, if it succeeded, would seal the fate of liberals and radicals alike. But instead of confronting the present crisis, the Left still babbles of revolution and looks to the Negroes, as before, to deliver the country from its capitalist oppressors. "We are just a little tail on the end of a very powerful black panther," says one of the delegates to the Conference for New Politics. "And I want to be on that tail—if they'll let me." In the next breath he urges white radicals to "trust the blacks the way you trust children."[7]

In this atmosphere, Harold Cruse's book, quite apart from its intrinsic and enduring merits, might do much immediate good. It might help to recall American radicals to their senses (those that ever had any). Perhaps it is too late

[7] Richard Blumenthal: "New Politics at Chicago," *The Nation*, September 25, 1967, p. 274. For other accounts of this fiasco see Andrew Kopkind: "They'd Rather Be Left," *New York Review of Books*, September 28, 1967, pp. 3–5; Dwight Macdonald in *Esquire*, December 1967, pp. 18 ff.; Renata Adler in *The New Yorker*, September 23, 1967, pp. 56 ff.; *The New York Times*, September 3, 1967; St. Louis *Post-Dispatch*, September 5, 1967. The best comment on the Conference for New Politics was written by James Ridgeway ("Freak-out in Chicago," *New Republic*, September 16, 1967, p. 12): "For some of us who have held out hope for the future of the radical political reconstruction in America, our despair was not so much in watching this fantasy as in quite suddenly realizing that neither the new nor the old left takes America seriously. Amidst the hilarity on the convention floor, a friend wrote to me two lines from Brecht: 'A man who laughs/Has simply not yet received the terrible news.' "

even for intelligent radicals to accomplish anything. *The Crisis of the Negro Intellectual* exposes the mistakes of the past at a time when the accumulated weight of those mistakes has become so crushing that it may be too late to profit from the lesson. Crises overlap crises. The defeat of liberal colonialism in Vietnam coincides with the defeat of liberalism in the ghetto, and the deterioration of the ghetto coincides with the deterioration of the city as a whole: the flight of industry and jobs from the city, the withdrawal of the middle class, the decay of public transportation and schools, the decay of public facilities in general, the pollution of the water, the pollution of the air.

In the 1930's an alarming crisis stirred enlightened conservatives like Franklin Roosevelt to measures which palliated the immediate effects of the crisis and thereby averted a general breakdown of the system. By throwing its support at a decisive moment behind the CIO, the New Deal made possible the organization of elements which, unorganized, threatened to become an immensely violent and disruptive force. One might imagine that the still graver crisis of the sixties might lead conservatives to consider a similar approach to the more moderate black nationalists. Indeed some gestures have recently been made in this direction. But given the total lack of national political leadership at the present time, and given the decay of the city, the kind of "solution" which will seem increasingly attractive to many Americans is a solution that would merely carry existing historical trends to their logical culmination: abandon the cities completely, put up walls around them, and use them as Negro reservations. This could even be done under the cloak of Black Power—"self-determination for the ghetto." On their reservations, black people would be encouraged to cultivate their native handicrafts, songs, dances, and festivals. Tourists would go there, bringing in a little loose change. In American history there are precedents for such "solutions."

Not only have things reached the point where any program of radical reform may be inadequate, it is still not clear whether even Cruse's version of black nationalism, as it stands, points the way to such a program. That the book itself offers no program is not an objection—although the objection applies, it seems to me, to Carmichael and Hamilton's *Black Power* which claims to present "a political framework and ideology which represents the last reasonable opportunity for this society to work out its racial problems short of prolonged destructive guerrilla warfare."[8] Cruse does not pretend to offer a "political framework"; his book attempts to clarify underlying issues. The question is whether his analysis clarifies those issues or obscures them.

That it clears up a great deal of confusion should already be evident. However, certain questions remain. One concerns the slippery concept of "nationalism," which may not be the best idea around which to organize a movement of Negro liberation. Cruse does not seem to me to confront the possibility that black nationalism, which he realizes has always been flawed by its "romantic and escapist" tendencies, may be *inherently* romantic and escapist—now looking wistfully back to Africa, now indulging in fantasies of global revolution.[9] The analysis of American Negroes as an ethnic group should properly include a study of the role of other nationalist ideologies, like Zionism or Irish-American nationalism, in order to discover whether they played any important part in the successful efforts of those communities to organize themselves. From what I have been able to

---

[8] Carmichael and Hamilton: *Black Power,* p. vi.
[9] Cruse: *The Crisis of the Negro Intellectual,* p. 82.

learn, Irish-American nationalism focused almost exclusively on Ireland and contributed nothing important to the political successes of the Irish in America.[1] A study of other ethnic nationalisms might show the same thing. It is possible, in other words, that nationalist movements in America, even when they cease to be merely fraternal and convivial and actually involve themselves in the revolutionary politics of the homeland (as was true of some Irish-American movements), have had no practical bearing on ethnic group politics in America itself. In that case, nationalism may not serve Negroes as a particularly useful guide to political action, although it is clear that the Negroes' situation demands some sort of action along ethnic lines.

Even as a means of cultural regeneration, nationalism may be too narrowly based to achieve what Cruse wants it to achieve. Black nationalist movements in the United States are largely movements of young men—of all groups, the one least able to develop values that can be passed on to the next generation. According to C. Eric Lincoln's study of the Black Muslims, "up to 80 per cent of a typical congregation is between the ages of seventeen and thirty-five"; moreover, "the Muslim temples attract many more men than women, and men assume the full management of temple affairs."[2] Frazier remarks, in another connection, "Young males, it will be readily agreed, are poor bearers of the cultural heritage of a people."[3] Of course there is no reason, in theory, why black nationalism should remain a young man's movement. The chief exponents of Negro-

[1] See Thomas N. Brown: *Irish-American Nationalism* (Philadelphia: J. B. Lippincott; 1966).
[2] Lincoln: *The Black Muslims in America*, pp. 22–3.
[3] Frazier: *The Negro Church in America*, p. 1.

American nationalism or of a point of view that could be called nationalist—Booker T. Washington, Garvey, and DuBois (when he was not swinging to the opposite pole of integration)—were themselves men of years and experience.

But historically the nationalist ideology has owed much of its appeal to the need of the young Negro male to escape from the stifling embrace of the feminine-centered family and church. The assertion of masculinity so obviously underlies the present manifestations of black nationalism that it is difficult, at times, to distinguish nationalist movements from neighborhood gangs. It is easy to see why black nationalism might be associated with riots, especially as nationalism becomes increasingly secularized and loses its capacity to instill inner discipline; but can it produce a culture capable of unifying the black community around values distinct from and superior to those of American society as a whole?

There is the further problem of what Cruse means by "culture." Sometimes he uses the word in its broad sense, sometimes narrowly, as when he asks Negro intellectuals to follow the lead of C. Wright Mills by formulating a theory of "cultural radicalism." In modern society, Cruse argues, "mass cultural communications is a basic industry," and "only the blind cannot see that whoever controls the cultural apparatus . . . also controls the destiny of the United States and everything in it."[4] This statement is open to a number of objections; but quite apart from that, it is not clear what it has to do with what Frazier called the Negro's "primary struggle"—to acquire a "culture" much more basic than the kind of culture Mills and Cruse, in this passage, have in mind. How are Negroes to get control of the

---

[4] Cruse: *The Crisis of the Negro Intellectual*, p. 474.

"cultural apparatus" until they have solved their more immediate difficulties? And how would their efforts to control the culture industry differ from the efforts of Lorraine Hansberry and Sidney Poitier, whom Cruse criticizes on the grounds that their personal triumphs on Broadway and in Hollywood did nothing to advance Negro "culture"?

These questions aside, Cruse leaves no doubt of the validity of his main thesis: that intellectuals must play a central role in movements for radical change, that this role should consist of formulating "a new political philosophy," and that in twentieth-century American history they have failed in this work. They must now address themselves to a more systematic analysis of American society than they have attempted before, building on the social theory of the nineteenth century but scrapping those parts that no longer apply. This analysis will have to explain, among other things, how the situation of the Negro in America relates to the rest of American history—a problem on which Cruse has now made an impressive assault, without, however, solving the dilemma posed by W. E. B. DuBois: "There faces the American Negro . . . an intricate and subtle problem of combing into one object two difficult sets of facts"—he is both a Negro and an American at the same time. The failure to grasp this point, according to Cruse, has prevented both integrationists and nationalists from "synthesizing composite trends."[5] The pendulum swings back and forth between nationalism and integrationism, but as with so many discussions among American intellectuals, the discussion never seems to progress to a higher level of analysis. Today riots, armed self-defense, conflicts over control of ghetto schools, efforts of CORE to move Negroes into cooperative communities in the South, and other uncoordinated actions,

[5] Ibid., p. 564.

signify a reawakening of something that can loosely be called nationalism; but they express not a new synthesis but varying degrees of disenchantment with integration. The advocates of Black Power have so far failed to show why their brand of nationalism comes any closer than its predecessors to providing a long-range strategy not for escaping from America but for changing it. The dilemma remains; more than ever it needs to become the object of critical analysis.

In the meantime, will events wait for analysis? Immediate crises confront us, and there is no time, it seems, for long-range solutions, no time for reflection. Should we all take to the streets, then, as Andrew Kopkind recommends? In critical times militancy may appear to be the only authentic politics. But the very gravity of the crisis makes it all the more imperative that radicals try to formulate at least a provisional theory which will serve them as a guide to tactics in the immediate future as well as to long-range questions of strategy. Without such a perspective, militancy will carry the day by default; then, quickly exhausting itself, it will give way to another cycle of disillusionment, cynicism, and hopelessness.

CHAPTER FIVE

THE REVIVAL OF POLITICAL CONTROVERSY IN THE SIXTIES

The ideological age has ended.
> —Daniel Bell, *The End of Ideology*

IN THE 1950'S, DANIEL BELL WAS ONLY ONE OF MANY
writers to proclaim the end of ideology—the end of
deep political conflict in the West, the end of utopian
attempts to reconstruct society. The editors of *Encounter,* in
a statement announcing the new magazine in 1953, gave
expression to the prevailing sense of living "after the apocalypse." Mussolini, Hitler, and now Stalin were dead. The
great upheavals of the first half of the twentieth century had
subsided; the ideologies that had moved masses had ex-
hausted themselves. Weary, sober, wise with the wisdom of
disillusionment, the survivors woke from the long night-
mare into homely reality, reassuring in its concreteness.
The cold gray morning light of midcentury dissipated the
last of the great abstractions. In East Germany and Czecho-
slovakia, *Encounter* observed, "the last surviving fable was
exposed . . . when real factory workers unambiguously dissociated themselves from a hypothetical proletariat, achiev-
ing by that simple action what a thousand subtle arguments
could not do." The age of argument had ended. "Now,
perhaps, we shall no longer be plagued by the rhetoric of a
messianic arrogance of the spirit which has blithely per-

petuated so many hideous crimes against the flesh."[1]

On the wreckage of the Soviet experiment grew a literature of disenchantment. Arthur Koestler's *Darkness at Noon* and George Orwell's *1984* became classics of the postwar period, penetrating deep into the postrevolutionary sensibility. The revolutionary hopes of an earlier generation now seemed to constitute a deep betrayal, treason not only to the national interests of the United States but to the basic values of Western civilization.

Yet the West had survived the storms that had threatened to destoy it. It had survived the Great Depression and the internecine struggle over fascism and emerged stronger than ever, prosperous and united. Its revival made old issues irrelevant. Utopianism and laissez-faire conservatism were alike discredited. "Few serious minds believe any longer," Daniel Bell observed, "that one can set down 'blueprints' and through 'social engineering' bring about a new utopia of social harmony. At the same time, the older 'counter-beliefs' have lost their intellectual force as well . . . In the Western world, therefore, there is today a rough consensus among intellectuals on political issues: the acceptance of a Welfare State; the desirability of decentralized power; a system of mixed economy and of political pluralism . . . The ideological age has ended."[2] Even radicals shared this view of capitalism as having achieved a remarkable stability. As late as 1964, Herbert Marcuse concluded that American society was so resistant to change that only revolutionary pressures from without could alter the prevailing system. "Contemporary society seems to be capable of containing social change. . . . This containment

---

[1] "After the Apocalypse," *Encounter*, October 1953, p. 1.

[2] Daniel Bell: *The End of Ideology* (New York: The Free Press of Glencoe; 1960), p. 373.

of social change is perhaps the most singular achievement of advanced industrial society."[3]

Only a few years later, all of Western society faces insurrectionary threats from within. Vietnam has exploded the cold-war consensus. The antiwar movement in the United States has grown to such proportions that it may prove impossible, in the future, to carry on American colonialism without resorting to wholesale repression at home.[4] Riots threaten to become a permanent feature of urban life. Militant black radicals openly proclaim their total disaffection from America and their solidarity with oppressed people in the Third World. All over the Western world students are in rebellion—in Berlin, in Rome, even in Madrid. In France students almost succeeded in bringing down a government many supposed to have been the most firmly established in the West.

It is clear now that the years of the cold-war consensus were only an interlude, a period of brief political quiescence marking the end of one stage of capitalist development and the beginning of another. The political issues and alignments of industrial society, the issues that dominated American politics from the end of the nineteenth century to the Second World War, have indeed become obsolescent. But we can see now that the commentators of the fifties and early sixties made the mistake of equating the obsolescence

[3] Herbert Marcuse: *One Dimensional Man* (London: Routledge & Kegan Paul; 1964), p. xii.

[4] "I suspect that if we get out of Vietnam we won't have much left in the way of a foreign policy." (Richard Rovere: "Half Out of Our Tree," *The New Yorker,* October 28, 1967, p. 99.) This seems a realistic assessment. The question is, however, whether those who guide our national destinies will be able to reconcile themselves to the loss of their global influence. On the other hand, efforts to continue the present policies would probably provoke a large-scale insurrection at home.

of certain political issues, peculiar to industrial society, with the obsolescence of all politics. Postindustrial society, however, generates new tensions peculiar to itself. It contains certain sources of conflict which cannot be divorced from the nature of the system; and these in turn give rise to a revival of ideology—that is, to political arguments in which both sides do not agree on the same premises.

Poverty, in postindustrial society, tends to become self-perpetuating and heritable. While the society as a whole becomes increasingly affluent, a large minority find themselves trapped in poverty. As their condition deteriorates, they become increasingly resentful and desperate, dangerously alienated from a system that is so easily able to function without them. Ethnic and racial divisions contribute to the explosiveness of the situation. Moreover, the masses of marginal poor now live concentrated in cities from which the new middle class and even the working class have escaped. The flight of these classes to the suburbs, followed by the flight of industry, signals the end of the urban age. Suburbanization reflects the decreasing dependence of industry on railroads and water transportation and on large reserves of unskilled labor, the vast growth of white-collar jobs in relation to the number of blue-collar jobs, and other changes associated with the passing of industrial society. To assess the full consequences of these changes would require an extended analysis of the American social order. Here it should be noted that the most explosive of these consequences is the predicament of new ethnic minorities left high and dry in a deteriorating environment, cut off from every access to the larger society either in the form of jobs, of opportunities in small business, or of education, which like all social services collapses with the demise of the city.

Another source of tension in what might be called postliberal capitalism is the university. In an advanced technological society, higher education for the first time becomes a mass industry, chiefly because of the unprecedented demand for highly trained personnel but also because in the United States a college degree has been somewhat arbitrarily defined as a requirement for high-status jobs, even where there is no demonstrable connection between the job and the training it is said to require; and it would be widely resented, therefore, if educational opportunities appeared to be arbitrarily restricted. Faced with a massive influx of students, higher education becomes increasingly bureaucratized and impersonal, increasingly oriented toward "production." Moreover, the universities are increasingly drawn into, and become dependent on, military research, research in counterinsurgency, and other activities of the state. At the same time the university remains a repository of humanistic learning and culture. The idea of the university as a privileged sanctuary for heretical ideas survives and still bears some resemblance to reality. Even though the university is no longer in any very meaningful sense a "community of scholars," there is still more freedom of speech and inquiry in the university than in American society as a whole, and a deeper commitment to values that run counter to those of the corporation and the corporate state.

There is a conflict, therefore, between the humane values of which the university is uniquely the embodiment and the knowledge factory. The university produces the technicians and the technical knowledge necessary to operate a highly developed technological society, but at the same time it produces opposition to its own bureaucratic character and to American society in general, the deficiencies of which are epitomized by the corruption even of so "privileged" an institution as the university. "The university is the place where people begin seriously to question the conditions of their existence." People "come to the university to learn to question, to grow, to learn—all the standard things that sound like clichés because no one takes them seriously." But the students find instead a bureaucratic institution organized for production. Mario Savio, leader of the Berkeley revolt, has observed, "The university is well structured, well tooled, to turn out people with all the sharp edges worn off, the well-rounded person. The university is well equipped to produce that sort of person, and this means that the best among the people who enter must for four years wander aimlessly much of the time questioning why they are on campus at all, doubting whether there is any point in what they are doing, and looking toward a very bleak existence afterward in a game in which all of the rules have been made up, which one cannot really amend."[5] The dual nature of the university generates conflicts so deep that they can no longer be hidden, as so many conflicts in American society are hidden, under a mask of benevolence. The university's very benevolence, its paternalism, comes under attack. "Paradoxically, the university offered its students the freedom to say much of what they wanted, as members of campus political clubs, and even to bring to the campus Communists and Nazis. But the [members of the Free Speech Movement at Berkeley] felt patronized by this approach, for to them it appeared that the university tolerated all of this talk as long as it did not interfere with the production of the educational corporation."[6]

[5] Mario Savio: "An End to History," in Seymour Martin Lipset and Sheldon S. Wolin, eds.: *The Berkeley Student Revolt* (Garden City: Anchor Books; 1965), pp. 218–19. On the Berkeley revolt see also Hal Draper: *Berkeley: The New Student Revolt* (New York: Grove Press; 1965); Michael V. Miller and Susan Gilmore, eds.: *Revolution at Berkeley* (New York: Dial Press; 1965).

[6] Paul Jacobs and Saul Landau: *The New Radicals* (New York: Random House; 1966), p. 60.

The effect of mass education changes the character not only of the university but of the student body as well. It removes masses of young people, at a critical period in their lives and for a considerable time, from the productive process and, more generally, from institutional ties to the rest of society. The university takes young people in great numbers from their families and from local and community affiliations, at a time when they have not yet acquired jobs, families of their own, property, or other ties to society. In traditional American education, fraternities and social clubs served as a way of tying students to family, class, and career; but these organizations, as is well known, are elitist in their style and tend to break down in the face of mass education. Thus postindustrial society creates, through the university, a new class of people who are "psychological adults," in Kenneth Keniston's term, but "sociological adolescents"—that is, adults who are wanting in "the prime sociological characteristic of adulthood: 'integration' into the institutional structures of society."[7]

These developments create the potential for a new radicalism. As marginal members of society, students as a class, like black people, are more likely than other classes to be attracted to perspectives highly critical of society, particularly when they are faced with "integration" into society in the form of the draft. This is the basic sociological condition that gives rise to the student Left and the "new radicalism" in general. More immediate influences, of course, have contributed to the revival of radicalism in the sixties. John Kennedy's presidency, coming after the long sleep of the Eisenhower years, may have contributed something to the reawakening of political impulses, especially among young

[7] Kenneth Keniston: *Young Radicals: Notes on Committed Youth* (New York: Harcourt, Brace & World; 1968), p. 260.

people; certainly his assassination did, since for many people it helped to dispel the illusion that the United States was somehow exempt from history, a nation uniquely favored and destined—or doomed, depending on one's point of view—to be spared the turmoil and conflict which had always characterized the politics of other countries. Meanwhile the civil rights movement in the South initiated a generation of students into radical politics. The students' experience in Georgia and Mississippi, combined with their experience in the Northern multiversity, led directly to the agitation which first flared up at Berkeley in 1964 and soon convulsed one campus after another. Even before Berkeley, Students for a Democratic Society, founded in 1960 under the auspices of the League for Industrial Democracy, broke away from its parent and in the Port Huron manifesto of 1962 proclaimed its alienation from a society allegedly dominated by the empty pursuit of personal success. Taking heart from these unexpected stirrings among students and black people (many of them students as well), remnants of the old Left—pacifists, Stalinists, Trotskyites, old-style socialists of one sort or another—began to emerge from the seclusion into which they had been driven by McCarthyism.

All these developments coincided with a new wave of revolutionary activity in the rest of the world, especially in the undeveloped countries, where movements of national liberation led by Castro, Ho Chi Minh, Mao Tse-tung, and others seemed to show that communism had by no means spent its revolutionary force. Dependent, as always, on foreign ideologies, the American Left rediscovered Marxism (insofar as it was attracted to Marxism at all) not through a new analysis of American society but through events abroad and through the writings of Che Guevara and Régis Debray. Marxism did not come back into fashion in the form into which it had evolved in other advanced countries

—that is, in the form of a body of doctrine that combined theoretical rigor with an insistence on mass action along democratic lines.[8] It surfaced again in the form of an ideology of intense activism aiming at the violent overthrow of colonialism by a guerrilla elite. Orthodox Marxism has had a very limited appeal for the young radicals of the sixties, partly because in their view it is plodding and unheroic, partly because they associate it with bureaucratic structures —whether embodied in political parties, corporations, or universities—which in turn are the principal objects of their anger. It is a peculiarity of the new radicals, as Arthur Waskow noted in 1965, that they "can in one breath damn the University of California as 'totalitarian' and deny that Cuba is"; but the contradiction disappears if bureaucracy itself, rather than some particular form of it, is defined as the target of radical politics. For the new radicals, Waskow observed, "Cuba seems to be 'turned on,' live, unbureaucratic, full of sex and unexpectedness, even if its government controls the press; but the multiversity is gray and chilly. Given a choice between repression and suppression, the students would choose to be suppressed."[9] These are hardly the accents of classical Marxism, as the Communists themselves were among the first to see when they attacked the New Left's "romantic revolutionary notions about violence and confrontation."[1]

---

[8] This tradition of Marxian thought, however, was maintained in the early sixties by the group of scholars (James Weinstein, Eugene D. Genovese, and others) around the journal *Studies on the Left*— an important exception to most of the generalizations one can make about the New Left.

[9] Arthur Waskow: "The New Student Movement," *Dissent*, p. 486.

[1] Bettina Aptheker, quoted in Michael Miles: "The Communist Party Today," *New Republic*, February 3, 1968, p. 23.

[II]

Both the strengths and the weaknesses of the New Left derive from the fact that it is largely a student movement based on "alienation." From the beginning, the New Left defined political issues as personal issues. How does one achieve personal integrity—"authenticity"—in a mechanized, bureaucratized, dehumanized society? In the fifties, the disaffection with modern life, already widespread, expressed itself as a retreat from the job into privacy. Young people confronted with the hierarchic, authoritarian, and repressive quality of established institutions gave to those institutions a purely formal allegiance, while saving what they hoped was the best of themselves for a life of intense domesticity. In effect, writes Christopher Jencks, "[We] wrote off the 9-to-5 portion of our lives" and "pinned most of our hopes on creating a comfortable and comforting family life which embodied the ideals we had picked up in our own childhoods."[2] In the sixties the same impulse takes the form of an attack on the institutions themselves. It takes the form of radical politics or, alternately, the hippie protest. But the issue of personal integrity remains. The Port Huron statement, for instance, declares that "men have unrealized potential for self-cultivation, self-direction, self-

---

[2] Christopher Jencks: "Is It All Dr. Spock's Fault?" *The New York Times Magazine*, March 3, 1968, p. 84. For an exhaustive study of alienated styles in the late fifties see Kenneth Keniston: *The Uncommitted: Alienated Youth in American Society* (New York: Harcourt, Brace & World; 1965). Reading Keniston, one cannot fail to be struck by the way certain themes carry over from the completely apolitical disaffection of the fifties to the political rebellion of the sixties. The cult of privacy has given way to the cult of "community," but the underlying values are much the same.

understanding, and creativity. . . . The goal of man and society should be human independence: a concern not with image or popularity but with finding a meaning in life that is personally authentic." It deplores the "loneliness, estrangement, and isolation" that "describe the vast distance between man and man today." In upholding "participatory democracy," it declares that "politics has the function of bringing people out of isolation and into community, thus being a necessary, though not sufficient, means of finding meaning in personal life." Turning to the question of the university, the Port Huron statement complains that the campus has become "a place of private people, engaged in their notorious 'inner emigration,'" where apathy "begets a privately constructed universe."³

These eloquent accusations define an undeniable reality. Charged, moreover, with deep moral feeling, they might have served as the starting point of political analysis. But they did not in themselves constitute an analysis, nor could they become the basis of radical politics. The search for personal integrity could lead only to a politics in which "authenticity" was equated with the degree of one's alienation, the degree of one's willingness to undertake existential acts of defiance. It is not too much to say that for some of the new radicals, "the important thing is to fail; to die nobly in the fight against fascism, while others destroy its imperialist foundations abroad. Success would be immoral as well as a bore."⁴ The obsession with authenticity, when combined with the genuine moral anguish of the war in Vietnam, generates a mystique of "resistance." "When we say resistance," writes a graduate student from Berkeley, "we mean just what we say: we want to close down the

---

³ Jacobs and Landau: *The New Radicals,* pp. 154–8.
⁴ Miles: "The Communist Party Today," p. 23.

induction centers, stop the troop trains, kick the recruiters off-campus, and generally shut the war machine down." He and his friends, however, "are under no illusion as to what the consequences of resistance will be. The resistance will be crushed." Resistance, in other words, becomes an act of pure desperation, "born of the knowledge that the situation is bad and getting worse."[5]

Acting out of an ideal of personal heroism rather than from an analysis of the sources of tension in American society and the possibilities for change, the New Left vacillates between existential despair and absurdly inflated estimates of its own potential. At the time of the Pentagon demonstration in October 1967, Carl Davidson of SDS wrote: "In general, we have been underestimating our own strength and overestimating the enemy." The demonstration against the Pentagon appeared to Davidson as an example of successful resistance. "The high point and victory of the resistance struggle occurred near dusk, after we had broken military lines, occupied THEIR TERRITORY, entered the Pentagon, and held our ground until the point where two of their soldiers came over to us."[6]

Originally devoted to nonviolence, the student Left increasingly admires violent "guerrilla" tactics—a consequence of frustration, of white students' efforts to keep up with the black movement, and of the continuing search for "authentic" styles of action. Many in the New Left now argue for a course that would invite repression so as to dramatize the brute force underlying the façade of consensus. At an SDS meeting in Princeton, a girl from Barnard argued: "We must polarize the government, the liberal's

[5] Richard J. Arneson to editor, Brown University *Daily Herald,* November 17, 1967.

[6] Carl Davidson: "Toward Institutional Resistance," SDS memorandum [1968], pp. 4–5.

government, against the majority. . . . Plan strategic interruptions which will force the government to increase its control over the people until they will not take it any more." At the same meeting another student, an anarchist, advocated a violent assault against the draft board in New York. "Sure the damn streets are narrow. But narrow streets demand new tactics. Throw grease on the streets. They will try to ride down the streets and club us. Those bastards from the Staten Island Ferry—the cops will let the fascist pigs fight us. They'll pour out of the subways once it starts. We'll burn. But we'll burn the streets first. We'll be hit but we'll hit the cops first. . . . It will be bloody but blood makes the liberals mad. And we've got to make them mad." A student from Rutgers drops even the pretense of tactics: "I'm a nihilist! I'm proud of it, proud of it! I want to fuck this goddam country. Destroy it! No hope, not in 50 years. Tactics? It's too late. You're dreamers. . . . Let's break what we can. Make as many answer as we can. Tear them apart."[7]

The nihilistic tendencies of the New Left might have been gradually modified by discussion, criticism, and political experience, if the Vietnamese war had not confronted the Left with its political impotence, thereby engendering a despair of patient efforts to create a broadly based radical movement. Even writers otherwise restrained and reasonable succumbed to the general sense of desperation. Mary McCarthy suggested that "if the opposition wants to make itself felt politically, it ought to be acting so as to provoke intolerance."[8] Even before the war there were signs that the

[7] Dotson Rader: "Princeton Weekend with the SDS," *New Republic,* December 9, 1967, pp. 15–16.

[8] Mary McCarthy: "Vietnam: Solutions," *New York Review of Books,* November 9, 1967, p. 6. Only in a country where political freedom was taken for granted could people talk so glibly about the

attack on corporate liberalism was degenerating, in the absence of a coherent program of radical alternatives, into indiscriminate attacks against the university and against "bourgeois civil liberties." The Free Speech Movement at Berkeley, as symptomatic in decline as in its ascendancy, after its initial victory in 1964 collapsed into a series of legalistic and meaningless confrontations with the administration, in which the demonstrators seemed to have had no clear object in mind other than harassment.[9] Once free speech had been established at Berkeley, it should have been used to raise important questions about the university, some of which, it is true, had been raised in connection with the free-speech agitation, but none of which had been systematically explored with an eye to making them the basis of political organization. Were students oppressed or disfranchised? Were they exploited in the same way black people are exploited? An article in the Los Angeles *Free Press* asserts that "students are niggers," that they "have separate and unequal dining facilities," that they are "politically disenfranchised," and that, in short, they "have no voice in the

---

tactical advantages of repression. Because political freedom is an essential condition of democratic socialism, it has always been one of the primary objectives of revolutionaries. Socialists have been forced to resort to violence precisely in the degree to which certain regimes proscribe democratic political organization. In a country where political freedom still exists—but where even now it is coming under increasing attack—undervaluation of civil liberties is a disastrous mistake. That these ideas should be advocated at all shows once again the characteristic failure of the Left to arrive at a proper assessment of the American situation. It also shows the new radicals' remoteness from the revolutionary tradition they claim to be defending.

[9] Sheldon S. Wolin and John H. Schaar: "Berkeley and the University Revolution," *New York Review of Books,* February 9, 1967, pp. 18–24.

decisions which affect their academic lives."[1] It might be objected, however, that authority and discipline are not necessarily instruments of oppression, and that in a university they serve quite different purposes from the purposes they serve on a plantation, say, or in a ghetto school. The whole question of "student power" raised intricate and difficult issues. Where did it fit into larger issues? Was student power part of a general strategy for creating a community of scholars which would be independent from industry and the military? Was the object of student power to detach the university from these connections, in the hope of altering the balance of political power in America by denying the military what had become a necessary resource? Or should the university become even more active in the community? Both the authors of the Port Huron statement and the Berkeley activists raised the question of military research, but it was not clear why they raised it, except as another example of liberal sell-out. It was not clear what they wished the university to become or what relation the reform of the university bore to the rest of society. It was not even clear that reform of the university was what the radicals wanted; many talked of "destroying" it without explaining, however, what they planned to put in its place.

At Berkeley the students might have capitalized on their free-speech victory by pressing on to these other issues. Instead they celebrated the triumph of free speech by proclaiming the stirring political slogan: "Fuck." Why should free speech have issued only in "fuck"? The new slogan could be counted on, presumably, to provoke the administration into reprisals; had that become an end in itself? The

---

[1] Quoted in *The Real Press* (Evanston, Illinois), January 22, 1968, p. 3.

suspicion grew that many of the new radicals were no more serious about the university than they were serious about anything else. It becomes more and more clear that many of them are so deeply alienated from American society that even the one institution that seems to many radicals to embody values transcending the present political system appears in their eyes as an absurdity.[2] One of the most striking documents of the New Left is Michael Rossman's "Notes from a California Jail," an article at once moving in its moral sensitivity and depressing, because of the cynicism and despair which are never far from the surface. Rossman, a veteran of the free-speech campaigns at Berkeley, compares the county jail to a university: both are forms of what he calls the authority complex. "If there's anything college teaches you," he writes, "it's how to relate to authority: even more than being black does, though the techniques are similar. . . . Establish a distinct but nonthreatening identity. . . . Pick a symbol of excellence in your subject; accentuate it. . . . Be passionately dedicated to the pursuit of truth; venture a daringly unorthodox hy-

---

[2] On the obscene speech campaign see Draper: *The New Student Revolt,* pp. 140–8. On the increasing contempt for the university among radicals, see J. M. Cameron's review of Norman O. Brown's *Love's Body (New York Review of Books,* May 4, 1967, p. 4), in which Cameron makes a criticism of Brown that has much wider application: "He does not value enough that ethos of the scholarly life which shows itself through all the shifts in the history of the academic consciousness, from the great moment when Abelard drew the young men of Europe to Paris by the sounding of the true music of the dialectic down to the modern period when the radiance of humble, arduous, tenacious scholarship shows itself . . . in the work of Ranke, Maitland, Tawney, Max Weber, and in the heroic and tragic dedication of (Brown's mentor) Sigmund Freud himself." In our own time the tradition of "humble, arduous, tenacious scholarship," together with the broader values it embodies, may be on the verge of disappearing once and for all.

pothesis whose subtle flaw the instructor can point out. . . . Admit an evident mistake gracefully; show yourself open to instruction and able to profit by it. . . . I could go on, but fuck it."[3] These lines are a commentary, to be sure, on the present state of the American university; but they are also a comment on the mentality that sees the pursuit of knowledge as principally an exercise in "relating to authority"— that and little more.

One must beware of exaggerating the nihilism of the New Left. The movement contains a variety of tendencies, none of which has clearly established its dominance. The fluidity and openness of the New Left organizations promote discussion and self-criticism. At the Princeton meeting on resistance, for example, the advocates of violence were vigorously challenged by those who argued that "demonstrations . . . simply alienate us from other people" and that radicals should "educate people first so that they understand what we are demonstrating against and why."[4] For every nihilist in the New Left, there are many more who are committed to long-term radical politics. What gives the militants an influence out of proportion to their numbers is that those committed to political action have not yet devised permanent forms through which organization and education could be carried out. Lacking such organizations, the New Left is condemned to the politics of protest, the very inconclusiveness of which generates an ever-accelerating demand for militant tactics. Student radicalism necessarily lacks continuity. "The New Left," writes Kenneth Keniston, "is almost entirely a movement of *young* men and women. . . . [It] has a high dropout rate, and most young radicals have left Movement work before they reach the age of thirty.

[3] Michael Rossman: "Notes from the County Jail," *New York Review of Books,* February 15, 1968, pp. 22–3.
[4] Rader: "Princeton Weekend with the SDS," pp. 15–16.

From those who wish to persist, organizing work generally demands an acceptance of subsistence wages and geographic mobility that is hard to combine with job and family." It should be noted that work in the movement is also hard to combine with serious intellectual work. "The New Left has yet to find ways for those who become involved in the conventional institutions of society to retain their active commitment to the Movement."[5] Under these conditions it is hard to avoid the suspicion that "ten years from now," as Hal Draper wrote of the eight hundred Berkeley students arrested for sitting-in at Sproul Hall, "most of them will be rising in the world and in income, living in the suburbs from Terra Linda to Atherton, raising two or three babies, voting Democratic, and wondering what on earth they were doing in Sproul Hall—trying to remember, and failing."[6] Until it solves the problem of continuity, the student Left will be a force for disruption but not, except indirectly, for major social change.

[III]

The New Left's chief contribution to American politics, so far, is that together with the war in Vietnam, it has moved many liberals several degrees leftward. Today the call for a "new politics" is sounded not only by radicals but by liberals opposed to the war and increasingly alarmed by the breakdown of representative goverment and the drift toward violence. Even though the Left itself has failed to

---

[5] Keniston: *Young Radicals,* pp. 260–1.
[6] Hal Draper: *Berkeley: The New Student Revolt* (New York: Grove Press; 1965), p. 169.

put together a movement capable of revolutionizing American society, it has communicated to many people a sense of crisis, an awareness of the system's unresponsiveness to their needs, which has turned them from admirers of American democracy into harsh critics.

On the ruins of the Conference for New Politics, which better than any other event illustrated the weakness, confusion, and incompetence of the New Left, there grew up another kind of new politics, scorned by the far Left but capable of organizing masses of voters, for a time, behind the campaigns of Eugene McCarthy and Robert Kennedy. Kennedy's assassination, appalling in itself, dramatized the condition which gave rise to these movements in the first place, the failure of the political system to function as it is supposed to function. The system no longer responds to the expressed wishes of the voters. If they elect Lyndon Johnson as a dove, he turns into a hawk; if they try to end the war by voting for Robert Kennedy, the arbitrary, unpredictable, and meaningless act of an assassin thwarts this choice as well. The nomination of Hubert Humphrey only drove home the point, leaving those who briefly caught a glimpse of hope despairing and embittered, and at the same time determined to carry on in some form the revolt against the Johnson policies which for a time promised to capture the Democratic party.

Since the "New Politics" promises to be with us for some time, it is important to ask whether it expresses anything more than opposition to the war, a growing concern about the divisions in American society, and a revolt against the present Democratic leadership. Some of the spokesmen for the antiwar movement and for democratic reform at home have begun to refer to themselves as "radical liberals" and to seek ways of extending liberalism beyond the cold-war consensus. They envision a new coalition of middle-class reformers, enlightened labor unions, students, and the poor, united behind a program of social change that would substantially alter American institutions while stopping short of revolution—an objective which the "radical liberals" consider unrealistic and probably undesirable as well. Their commitment to work within the existing political system distinguishes them from the militant leaders of the New Left, with whom, however, they share a dissatisfaction with the present state of American society so deep that it is unlikely they could be reconciled to a continuation of the old politics. As a new element in American politics, therefore, "radical liberalism" deserves careful attention. Is it capable of becoming a new majority? And if it did become a new majority, would it be capable of democratizing America?

Two recent books—Arnold Kaufman's *The Radical Liberal* and Michael Harrington's *Toward a Democratic Left* —can be read as manifestoes of the new movement. Together they show some of the potentialities and limitations of the "new man in American politics"—the man who recognizes that liberalism can save itself, in Kaufman's words, only by "a resolute turn toward radicalism."[7] By a turn toward radicalism, however, Kaufman means only that liberal rhetoric must be squared with liberal practice. He thinks that liberalism, with its emphasis on individual liberty and "rational choice," still "possesses moral and intellectual resources richer than those of any competing tradition."[8] This dubious statement is defended on purely philosophical grounds. (Kaufman is a philosopher by profession, and one of the founders of the teach-in movement.) He

---

[7] Arnold S. Kaufman: *The Radical Liberal: New Man in American Politics* (New York: Atherton Press; 1968), p. 3.

[8] Ibid., p. 2.

shows that the liberal tradition embodies enduring aspirations and insights, but he does not demonstrate that they can provide a way out of the present darkness. Indeed he does not even demonstrate, except by wholly spurious comparisons, that these aspirations and insights are peculiar to liberalism. It is true that "liberal emphasis on the importance of liberty and human rights, and the corresponding sensitivity to the danger of tyrannical abuse of corporate power, has resulted in an insistence on the fundamental value of political democracy." But it is not true that "this conviction marks the most important difference between liberalism and Marxist humanism."[9] Many Western Marxists have absorbed these values; they differ from liberals not in holding political democracy in contempt but in asserting that political democracy in itself—even assuming that it existed in the United States—does not prevent class rule. This assertion would have to be successfully refuted before one could agree with Kaufman that the conflicts, injustices, and violence that now pervade American society derive not from the inherent inadequacies of liberalism but from the failure to put liberal principles into practice.

Kaufman's argument throughout is pitched at a level of vague abstraction that enables him to reconcile contradictory points of view and thereby to prove that "radicalism" is merely a logical extension of liberalism—and not a criticism of some of its leading assumptions. If it is objected that parliamentary democracy lends itself to manipulation by elites, Kaufman reminds us that "participatory democracy," after all, is itself part of the liberal tradition. Participatory democracy and "coalition politics" should be combined: *"both* are essential."[1] If it is objected that the civil rights

[9] Ibid., pp. 8–9.
[1] Ibid., p. 60.

movement failed to solve the race problem, Kaufman agrees with the criticism—"it is certain that only a minority actually received significant aid during the last decade of effort"—but then goes on to suggest that "the central tendencies of the Black Power Movement are liberal" and that what the country needs, therefore, is a judicious mixture of civil rights agitation (even though it failed) and Black Power (although separatism is of course unthinkable). "Conventional civil rights activity has accomplished much; it has much yet to accomplish. There is plenty of room for people who, by temperament or aptitude, can do their best work in the new or the old."[2]

Fond of reconciling irreconcilables, Kaufman is forever exhorting his readers to avoid "either-or's."[3] He spends much of his time cautiously steering between extremes. On the one hand he denounces the "pseudo-realism" of those liberals, for instance, who insist on knowing what critics of the war would do if *they* were in the President's place; on the other hand he attacks the politics of "self-indulgence," which preserves radical purity at the expense of political effectiveness. His criticisms of both positions are well taken but irrelevant to the question of whether his own radical liberalism is adequate to the crisis of American society. An affirmative answer to this question demands more than a criticism of "defective political styles"; it demands a rigorous analysis of American institutions which would show that they are capable of the kind of change Kaufman thinks is necessary.

In place of analysis he offers vapid generalities. "Again and again Marxists and socialists have had to learn that the institutions of countries like the United States are resilient

---

[2] Ibid., pp. 77, 104.
[3] Ibid., p. 104.

enough to defeat their ominous predictions." "Even if a power elite exists, there is little reason to suppose that its members have identical interests or even perceive developments in precisely the same ways." "For all its defects, American society is progressive in the perspective of history."[4] The validity of these assertions is by no means self-evident.

Michael Harrington's book, on the other hand, contains much critical analysis. He calls for radical changes, but since he expects them to be carried out within existing political structures, he should be understood as advocating, like Kaufman, a radicalized liberalism. The difference between them is that Harrington makes a serious effort to show that such a movement could grow out of the existing situation and that it would be capable of solving existing problems.

Up to a point, Harrington's analysis derives from John Kenneth Galbraith's *The New Industrial State*. Like Galbraith, he argues that there are two economies in the United States, the economy dominated by large corporations commanding advanced technology and therefore relatively independent of the market, and the old-fashioned market economy where "one finds transients, such as migrant farm laborers and casual restaurant employees, and the steady workers in the shops of cockroach capitalism."[5] Affluence in the one coexists with chronic depression and unemployment in the other. The corporation has evolved from an entrepreneurial to a bureaucratic institution, and now exercises *de facto* planning authority. Because this planning is dictated by private rather than social objectives, the industrial system has brought the country to the edge of disaster.

[4] Ibid., pp. 162, 163, 52.
[5] Michael Harrington: *Toward a Democratic Left: A Radical Program for a New Majority* (New York: Macmillan; 1968), p. 59.

The point at which Harrington departs from Galbraith is the latter's contention that the modern corporation "brings into existence, to serve its intellectual and scientific needs, the community that, hopefully, will reject its monopoly of social purpose."[6] According to Galbraith, the intellectual and scientific community, working through the universities and the state, will demand that, since corporations are already public bodies in effect, they should be treated "as a detached and autonomous arm of the state," necessary for efficient production "but responsive to the larger purposes of the society." Meanwhile the members of the corporate "technostructure," having absorbed the liberalizing influence of the universities in which they are trained, and no longer concerned in their jobs with maximizing profits, will come to see the corporation in the same way, "as an essentially technical arrangement for providing convenient goods and services in adequate volume."[7] The industrial system will thus be corrupted from within at the same time that it is subjected to increasing control from without.

Harrington thinks this is "just a bit too hopeful." It is irrelevant, in his opinion, whether the corporate manager's power rests on property or expert knowledge. "As an institutional entity, as a whole, the corporation acts like a throwback."[8] Harrington is surely right about this, in general. Even if the corporation is not strictly speaking a throwback, it should be noted that Galbraith's own analysis shows that the new corporate goal of "more efficient production"—that is, growth—comes to the same thing, for many social purposes, as the maximization of profits. "So-

[6] John Kenneth Galbraith: *The New Industrial State* (Boston: Houghton Mifflin; 1967), p. 399.

[7] Ibid.

[8] Harrington: *Toward a Democratic Left,* pp. 114, 119.

cial thought in the industrial system does not allow of inquiry as to whether increased or more efficient production of a particular product is a good thing. It is, *per se,* a good thing."[9] In *The Affluent Society* Galbraith attacked precisely this mystique of growth and noted its hold not only on corporate managers but on the presumably enlightened members of society—the "intellectual and scientific estate" which in his more recent book he sees as the main hope of social change.

Harrington correctly concludes that new elites will not become the agents of democratic progress. "If the scientific and educational estate were to make more and more decisions, but in the absence of a dynamic political movement asserting its own democratic priorities, these refined and sincere men would turn out to be the servants of the old values refurbished rather than the creators of new values."[1] The same phenomenon on which Galbraith builds his hope of change—the emergence of a community of technicians and experts moving back and forth between industry, the university, and the federal government—Harrington sees as sinister. Whereas Galbraith expects the values of the university to prevail over those of the industrial system, Harrington thinks it more likely that the "social-industrial complex" will take over the university. Thus the expansion of the communications industry—IBM, Xerox, CBS—into the educational market is a portent that "fundamental decisions about learning will become a function of the corporate struggle for shares of the knowledge market."[2] And the universities' subservience to the "military-industrial complex" is too well known to require further comment.

[9] Galbraith: *The New Industrial State*, p. 348.
[1] Harrington: *Toward a Democratic Left*, p. 115.
[2] Ibid., p. 90.

Notwithstanding these criticisms of Galbraith, Harrington does not reject the possibility that "a new class is coming into being," composed of "scientists, technicians, teachers and professionals in the public sector of the society."[3] This possibility, he reminds us, has been advanced not only by liberals like Galbraith and David Bazelon but (in somewhat different form) by writers on the New Left, who talk of a new white-collar proletariat.[4] The new class, however, will not make itself felt, as Galbraith and Bazelon believe, as "a subversive and conspiratorial underground inside the corporate structure." Nor will it automatically evolve into a force for democratic change. On the contrary, the "profound ambiguity in this emerging social formation" is that it tends as much toward state socialism, as Louis Boudin predicted years ago, or toward "liberalized totalitarianism," in Harrington's words, as toward a radicalized liberalism.[5]

The new class can become a democratic influence only if it operates outside the existing structures of economic power, and only if it allies itself with the poor and the unions. Here is another difference between Harrington's conception of the new class and the Galbraith-Bazelon thesis, which either sees no radical potential in these groups

[3] Ibid., p. 290.

[4] See David T. Bazelon: *Power in America: The Politics of the New Class* (New York: New American Library; 1967) and my review in *New York Review of Books*, September 28, 1967, pp. 12–14. For discussion of the white-collar proletariat on the Left see Gregory Calvert: "In White America: Radical Consciousness and Social Change," *National Guardian*, March 25, 1967, pp. 3–4; Manuel Bridier: "New Working Class or New Bourgeoisie," *International Socialist Journal*, January–February 1966, pp. 3–13; Lelio Basso: "Old Contradictions and New Problems," ibid., July 1966, pp. 235–54.

[5] Harrington: *Toward a Democratic Left*, p. 286; Louis Boudin: *The Theoretical System of Karl Marx* (Chicago: Charles H. Kerr; 1920 [1st edn. 1907]), p. 210.

or ignores them altogether. Whereas the Galbraith-Bazelon version of the "new class" theory is characterized by a misguided faith in the creative function of elites, Harrington's seems to point toward a new populism based on a coalition of poor people, whose "material self-interest . . . can be satisfied only through united political action," and the new middle class, "which could well have a non-material interest in basic change." Harrington does not deny the difficulties of bringing these groups together, but he thinks that a "rational" assessment of their interests ought to unite them.[6]

Recent events provide some support for this analysis. In his primary campaigns Robert Kennedy won votes both from Negroes and from the white working class (though not from the labor leadership), while McCarthy commanded impressive support in what Harrington calls the "conscience constituency" of middle class liberals.[7] Taken together these two movements roughly correspond to Harrington's new coalition. On the other hand, the course of the campaign provides little support for Harrington's belief that such a coalition can capture the Democratic party, purge it of reactionary elements, and turn it into an instrument of "democratic planning." Even before Kennedy's murder, it was becoming more and more obvious that the party leaders, who still maintain effective control, preferred the old politics to the new. Moreover, the Kennedy-McCarthy coalition, at the time of Kennedy's death, had still failed to coalesce; and this failure reflected not only personal rancor between the two leaders but the deeper problem of uniting such disparate political elements.

Finally, even if such a coalition had emerged, and even if

[6] Harrington: *Toward a Democratic Left,* p. 266.
[7] Ibid., p. 291.

it had captured the party, there was no indication that it was a coalition based on deep popular commitment to "democratic planning." Neither Kennedy (whom Harrington backed) nor McCarthy indicated support even for the "Freedom Budget," which Harrington admits is a minimal reform.[8] (The fact that, in the context of current politics, even this appears hopelessly utopian is a measure of our desperate situation.) "The strategy of massive public investments and of governmental persuasion of the private sector [to construct model cities, etc.] can be put into effect at once," Harrington writes. "They already command the support of a potential new majority in the civil-rights, labor, liberal and religious movements." But this assessment of the political scene also appears "just a bit too hopeful."[9] In the end, his optimism is no better founded than any other optimistic predictions about the immediate future of American politics.

The trouble is that Harrington's analysis stops short of the conclusion to which it logically leads. He is correct in saying that there are no new social forces automatically evolving toward socialism (which is what "democratic planning" comes down to). Presumably this means that radical change can only take place if a new political organization, explicitly committed to radical change, wills it to take place. But Harrington backs off from this conclusion. Instead he seems to predicate his strategy on the wistful hope that socialism will somehow take over the Democratic

[8] Advocated by Bayard Rustin, A. Philip Randolph, and others, the "Freedom Budget" would allocate $185 billion over a ten-year period for slum clearance, housing, public works, generation of new job opportunities, and in general "for the obliteration of poverty." See Bayard Rustin: *Which Way Out?* (League for Industrial Democracy Occasional Papers, No. 9), p. 11.

[9] Harrington: *Toward a Democratic Left,* p. 141.

party without anyone realizing what is happening. He admits that "there is obvious danger when those committed to a new morality thus maneuver on the basis of the old hypocrisies." But there is no choice, because radicals cannot create a new movement "by fiat." It is tempting, Harrington says, to think that the best strategy for the Left might be to "start a party of its own." But this course would not work unless there were already an "actual disaffection of great masses of people from the Democratic Party."[1]

At this point, however, one has to ask whether large defections from a liberal to a socialist party would be likely to occur in the absence of a socialist alternative. People do not defect from existing parties unless there is some place to defect to. Until the Left creates "a party of its own," defectors will have no place to go, except perhaps to occasional third-party movements based on single issues. Thus the McCarthy movement—what remains of it—cannot become the nucleus of a new radical majority unless the discontent it reflects is given more radical direction. In its present form the movement is not a force for radicalism for the simple reason that it has not committed itself to radical principles.

Radical change, as Harrington himself makes clear in refuting theories of the automatic evolution toward socialism, can only come about through radical consciousness. But how is this consciousness to be created except through a political organization which embodies it, and which dares to call things by their proper names?

It is true, as Harrington says, that "before raising the barrier of a new party . . . there must be some reasonable expectation that significant forces will join it."[2] There is, of course, no immediate prospect that a majority of Ameri-

---

[1] Ibid., pp. 294–5.
[2] Ibid., p. 295.

cans would support a socialist party. In order to arrive at an accurate assessment of what this prospect means, however, one must realize that the object of a radical party is not primarily to win elections, to register a protest vote, or to influence the major parties, as American third parties have traditionally done, but to introduce socialist perspectives into political debate, to create a broad consciousness of alternatives not embraced by the present system, to show both by teaching and by its own example that life under socialism would be preferable to life under corporate capitalism, and thus *in the long run* to fashion a new political majority.

In the short run, the success of a new party would depend not on huge electoral victories but on its capacity to gather to itself the widespread discontent that already exists and to furnish it with more enduring forms of expression than either third-party campaigns on the one hand or the existing organizations of the New Left on the other can hope to provide. Neither political campaigns nor protest demonstrations enable people with knowledge and skills to participate in radical politics except as protestors and campaign workers. Those people continue to devote the better part of their lives to work in existing institutions, even though they find much of that work unrewarding. What are needed—and there is a growing awareness of this among those who are talking about a new party—are institutions that would parallel existing structures of government (city councils, for instance) and, without any recognized authority or immediate hope of implementing their decisions, undertake the social planning of which the existing institutions are incapable. In other words the Left has to begin to function not as a protest movement or a third party but as an alternative political system, drawing on the abilities of people who realize that their talents are often wasted in their present jobs. It has to generate analysis and plans for action in which people of varying commitments to radicalism can take part, while at the same time it must insist that the best hope of creating a decent society in the United States is to evolve a socialism appropriate to American conditions.

A party capable of bringing such a movement into existence would have to be an once disciplined and democratic, nonsectarian and at the same time firmly committed to certain basic principles and programs, militant without making a cult of militancy. Whether it is possible to synthesize all these conflicting tendencies is a good question, but it is not the same question as asking whether the potential constituency for a radical party represents "significant forces" in American life. The latter question can be answered, with some confidence, in the affirmative. Without for a moment falling in with the leftist delusion that a minority can make a revolution in the United States, one can say that the basis for a new politics going well beyond "radical liberalism" already exists. The dissident movements ranging from the McCarthy and Kennedy campaigns to the militants of the student and black Left have revealed wide areas of discontent not only with the old political leadership but with the general quality of American life. The immediate constituency for a radical movement, it is clear, lies in the professions, in sections of suburbia, in the ghetto, and above all in the university, which more than any other institution has become a center of radicalism.

The university is a radicalizing influence in American life not because it gives rise to a scientific and intellectual elite which is devoted to democratic planning, nor because there is a "correlation between high educational attainment and libertarian views" as Harrington notes,[3] but because

[3] Ibid., p. 289.

changes in the social function of higher education have made the university itself a major focus of political conflict. It is a mistake to imagine that the university produces a superior breed of people and that these people, diffused throughout American society, will gradually make their influence felt on the side of political enlightenment. Even if it were true that the university is bringing into being a "conscience community," this community would have little power to change the corporate institutions to which in any case the interests of many conscientious people are firmly tied.

What matters is what is happening *within* the university —the conflict between the university's role as center of free thought and its corruption by the government, the corporations, and the military. This conflict gives rise to student radicalism. As noted, their very marginality predisposes radical students to cultivate a radicalism of alienation, of nihilistic gestures, of hysterical militancy. Student radicalism, being university-based, suffers from the additional disadvantage of identifying the university as the major enemy, thereby obscuring the fact that it is precisely the tension in the university, between its corruption by outside influences and its continuing independence from them, that creates the possibility of a radical movement in the first place. The *Berkeley Barb* shrilly proclaims that "the universities cannot be reformed" and calls for guerrilla bands to sweep through "college campuses burning books, busting up classrooms, and freeing our brothers from the prison of the university."[4]

The student Left is not inherently romantic and nihilistic, but it will probably continue to suffer from these tendencies

[4] Quoted in Benjamin DeMott: "The Age of Overkill," *The New York Times Magazine,* May 12, 1968, p. 104.

until it finds ways "for those who become involved in the conventional institutions of society," as Keniston puts it, to go on functioning as part of the movement. The search for more durable forms of organization would be necessary in any case, because a purely student movement necessarily lacks continuity. It also lacks the skills, plans, programs, theory, and "ideology" that are necessary to the development of alternatives, without which even a fundamental crisis in American society would not necessarily lead to the modification of the present system. All these things can be provided only by a revolutionary party, in its earlier stages largely based on students, disaffected faculty, professionals, and other middle-class dissidents, but defining itself not as a movement of people under thirty but as a prospective majority—a party of all those whose lives are now controlled by decisions in which they have no part.

Radicalized liberalism, as represented by Kaufman and Harrington, is no substitute for a radical party. Nevertheless the emergence of a dissident liberalism, which found at least a temporary home in the McCarthy movement, is an important and heartening development. It may be the only political force strong enough to save the country from a general reaction, in which even the possibility of change would be lost for generations to come. No matter what some militants think, a mass movement for radical change cannot grow up in a setting of repression.[5] It demands that the avenues of discussion remain open, that limits be placed on the powers of the secret police and other agencies of

[5] On this point see my exchange with Staughton Lynd, *New York Review of Books,* September 12, 1968, pp. 42–3. Lynd argues that "the *only* occasions on which developed societies have come to the point of revolutionary crisis have been . . . 'settings of repression.'" In support of this curious contention he cites "Germany in 1918, France and Italy in 1944, France in 1968." That is, he cites examples

"law enforcement," and that the freedom to convince and persuade, in short, be protected both from vigilantes and from official attacks. So long as the "radical liberal" remains committed to the defense of these principles, he is the ally, not the enemy, of those who are seeking a deeper reconstruction of American life. Essential liberties have survived even in our flawed democracy. If these are destroyed, liberals and radicals will go down together.

---

of abortive movements (a) which were not revolutionary, since they failed precisely because in each case the rebels had no plan or even any intention of taking power, and (b) which in any case cannot be said to have occurred during repression. On the contrary—and this holds true for successful revolutions as well as for the failures from which Lynd wishes to draw comfort and support—they took place at precisely the moment when repressive regimes, owing to military defeat, internal dry rot, and other debilitating influences, had lost their capacity to repress. On the other hand, revolutionary movements have repeatedly been stifled by repression, as in Russia at various times in the nineteenth century, in all of Europe after 1848, or in Italy under Mussolini—a particularly notable example because the Italian Communists, following a line of argument similar to the one now advocated by Lynd, contributed to their own undoing by refusing to join bourgeois elements in resisting fascism while there was still time.

Radicals have everything to lose from repression. Lynd's indifference to the dangers ahead strikes me as ill-informed and irresponsible. It arises not only from his misreading of history, particularly the history of revolutionary movements, but from the delusion, quite common on the New Left, that a minority of committed activists can make a revolution in an advanced country.

POSTSCRIPT: AFTER THE
CHICAGO CONVENTION, 1968

Ever since the cold war began, the Center in American politics has increasingly had to adopt the policies and outlook of the right. Thus the Truman administration, after first ridiculing the rightist myth of an internal communist conspiracy, set up a loyalty program based on the premise that this myth was a reality. Similarly the Eisenhower administration outmaneuvered Joseph McCarthy by making his anticommunist crusade official policy, in the form of Attorney General Brownell's security program. In foreign policy, liberals of the Center adopted as their own the theory that militant communism, bent on world domination, had to be contained by armed force, even though the policy of containment, as originally formulated by George F. Kennan, had not been intended to be exclusively military in its emphasis. When right-wing politicians launched their hysterical attack against Castro, Kennedy obliged them, in spite of his own last-minute misgivings, with the Bay of Pigs. When Goldwater demanded the liberation of South Vietnam, Johnson denounced him as a demagogue while secretly (and later not so secretly) putting Goldwater's foreign policy into practice.

The dynamics of cold-war politics demanded of centrist liberals a continual effort to outmaneuver the Right by preempting it. This strategy, however, far from putting down the Right, merely contributed to its amazing growth. In taking over so much of the rightist program, liberal politi-

cians raised expectations they were incapable of satisfying—
victory in Korea, victory in Vietnam, the defeat of the revolutionary movement all over the world. Instead of appeas-
ing the Right, the inconclusive policy of containment encouraged clamor for the liberation of "captive nations,"
while at home, the unsuccessful attempt to contain explosive forces for change generated a rising demand for their
forcible suppression. This demand now threatens to engulf
the Center itself.

After twenty years of the cold war, the focus of American politics has shifted far to the right. The liberal strategy
of maintaining economic growth through arms spending, of
containing revolution through a series of limited police actions, and of buying off domestic discontent by building
superhighways and cars by means of which the newly prosperous ethnic constituencies, still the backbone of the
liberal-welfare coalition, could escape the cities to the con-
sumer paradise of the suburbs—this strategy fell apart against
the unexpected obstacles of Vietnam, ghetto riots, and student rebellion. Not until Chicago, however, did its utter
bankruptcy stand fully revealed. The Democratic debacle in
Chicago showed, in the starkest terms, that the cold war can
no longer be maintained under the guise of liberalism;
showed, more broadly, that the corporate order can defend
itself against its combined opponents within and without
only by calling in the assistance of the most reactionary
forces in American life. What other meaning can we assign
to the savagery with which the Chicago police, unrestrained
by their nominal superiors, set upon not only the peace
demonstrators but reporters, bystanders, and finally even
the delegates themselves?[6] In Chicago and elsewhere the

[6] See *Newsweek*, September 9, 1968, pp. 38–41; *Life*, September
6, 1968, pp. 18 ff.; *Village Voice*, September 5, 1968, pp. 23–35;

police are no longer merely agents of corporate liberalism, they have become a political force in their own right, a force that has to be appeased. The brutal events in Chicago, the systematic harassment of the Black Panthers in Oakland, the unprovoked attack on black militants in a Brooklyn courthouse by off-duty policemen openly sympathetic to George Wallace, all testify to an emerging pattern of unofficial violence that has penetrated deep into official institutions. The police in American cities, like the Green Berets and other military elites charged with the repression of subject populations, have developed a colonial psychology manifesting itself in contempt for civilian values and the rule of the politicians. Sections of the police have developed what can only be called a fascist mentality, which corresponds, moreover, to anxieties among workers and the petit-bourgeoisie that are already preparing these classes for an American version of fascism. The brutal suppression of riots and demonstrations evokes an instinctive sympathy among "little people," as Wallace calls them, whose hard-won gains now seem threatened on the one side by Negroes and on the other by encroachments of the federal government. The congruence of semi-official violence with the racist violence of the mob in order to produce a fascist reaction requires only a crisis so grave—a full-scale uprising of the ghettos, an economic breakdown, another Vietnam,—that the dominant powers in America, backed by a hysterical populace, would be willing in their panic to turn away from politicians like Nixon and Humphrey, who retain some lingering commitment, however tenuous, to democratic procedures, and to embrace leaders who prom-

---

ise to stop at nothing in the restoration of law and order.

The McCarthy-Kennedy movement represented what may prove to have been the last chance to maintain the American empire under liberal auspices, by cutting its losses in Vietnam, diverting money into the ghetto, and providing young people with a plausible outlet for their dissatisfaction with the emptiness of American life. Not only the fact but the manner of Humphrey's nomination— the refusal to compromise on the Vietnam plank; the silencing of dissenting voices from the floor; the packing of the hall with Daley forces; the harassment of McCarthy delegates; the cruel battle waging in the streets while Humphrey sat undistracted before the televised unreality of the roll call; above all, Humphrey's refusal to disavow the actions of Daley's thugs—all these things make clear the price that must now be paid by those wishing to carry on the politics of American world power. The price in repression will mount as the cities and campuses erupt in despairing violence. In the 1968 campaign the Republicans, already sensing the shape of things to come, devised a "Southern strategy" to counter what they correctly perceived to be the only serious threat to their campaign—not the peace movement, which earlier in the year seemed destined to play an important if not decisive part in the outcome, but the Wallace candidacy. With New York and California virtually unrepresented in either party, the South, together with the reactionary industrial states of Ohio, Michigan, Pennsylvania, Indiana, and Illinois, emerged as the major battleground of the 1968 elections.

It is clearer than ever that radicalism is the only long-term hope for America. The erosion of the liberal Center makes it difficult for liberals to undertake even palliative reforms. This is why liberals like Arnold Kaufman realize that liberalism can save itself only by making an alliance with radicalism—whether in the new party, a restructured Democratic party, or in some other form will be the subject of much debate among radical-liberals. A radicalized liberalism under a leader like Ted Kennedy or John Lindsay might force concessions to the Negroes, forestall disastrous military adventures abroad, turn back the right-wing assault against the Warren court and against civil liberties in general, and thereby postpone the collapse of liberal capitalism. In the long run, however, liberalism cannot eliminate the contradictions of that system. It cannot liquidate the overseas empire or liberate the cities, because these things require the destruction of the power of great corporations—the oil industry, the auto industry, the insurance companies, the makers of armaments, to name only a few—which profit from existing arrangements. If America is to become a democracy, the only question is whether the power of these corporations can be destroyed piecemeal—for example, by creating autonomous enclaves of socialism in the ghettos and elsewhere—or whether it will be destroyed only through some ultimate confrontation in the future. Liberalism does not address itself to this question; it proposes only an extension of the welfare state. Nor does it address itself to the disintegration of values, the alarming spread of nihilism and alienation, which is bound up with the social and economic crisis of liberal capitalism. The liberal values of self-reliance, sexual self-discipline, ambition, acquisition, and accomplishment, while often admirable in themselves, have come to be embodied in a social order resting on imperialism, elitism, racism, and inhuman acts of technological destruction. They have therefore lost their capacity to serve as a guide to any but individual conduct. As a social philosophy, liberalism is dead; and it cannot survive even as a private morality unless it is integrated into a new moral and philosophical synthesis beyond liberalism. Such a synthesis, it seems clear, will emerge only in connection with a political movement that tries to demonstrate, both in practice and theory, how the unprecedented technological achievements of postindustrial society can become the basis for a new order in which men will no longer be slaves to production.

Radicalism—socialism—is the only long-term hope; but the almost overwhelming difficulties confronting the radical movement in America are suggested, more clearly perhaps than by anything else, by the vagueness and imprecision of the term "socialism." What is "socialism," particularly in an advanced country? For most Americans, the word has ugly overtones of bureaucracy, centralization, and forcible repression. Nor is this unjustified or surprising, considering the nature of most of the existing socialist regimes. Because socialism first came to power not in the seat of industrialism, as Marxian theory assumed it would, but in countries where the material basis for a socialism of abundance did not yet exist, twentieth-century socialist regimes have had to address themselves first of all to the task of capital accumulation— a task that in the West was performed by capitalism itself. For this reason if for no other, socialist regimes in undeveloped countries cannot serve as models for advanced countries. Their very existence, however, has helped to impede the development of socialist theory and programs appropriate to advanced industrial societies, since it was always easier, as we have seen throughout these essays, for Western socialists to import a ready-made theory than to fashion one of their own. The blinding prestige of the Russian and later the Chinese revolution tended to conceal not only the monstrous character of Stalinism but its total irrelevance to the attempt to build socialism in the West.

When they have not patterned themselves after irrelevant (and often barbarous) examples, those who call themselves socialists in the advanced countries have tended to become social democrats, indistinguishable in most essential respects from welfare liberals. Where they are in power, as in Sweden and Great Britain, social democrats not only offer no alternative to capitalism that is relevant to the needs of advanced countries—something they share with socialists in the undeveloped countries—they offer no alternative at all. Where they are out of power, the social democrats form a loyal opposition that breaks down completely at just those moments when an opposition is most needed. Beginning with the First World War, social democrats in the West have been among the staunchest defenders of imperialism; and even those who oppose imperialism have offered no plausible strategy for putting an end to it.

Socialism in the West oscillates between capitulation and a mindless revolutionary militancy based on irrelevant models. The New Left in America, in spite of its ostensible repudiation of Stalinism and other ideologies of the 1930's, is no exception to this generalization. It is true that the New Left has articulated values, derived for the most part from an indigenous tradition of radical populism, that might become the basis of a new socialism addressing itself to the needs of the twentieth century, not to those associated with the early stages of capital accumulation. In espousing decentralization, local control, and a generally antibureaucratic outlook, and by insisting that these values are the heart of radicalism, the New Left hs shown American socialists the road they must follow. Until American socialism identifies itself with these values, it will have nothing to offer either to black people or to all those others whose suffering derives not merely from the private ownership of the means of production but from the dehumanizing effects of bureaucratic control.

The history of the New Left, however, shows what can happen when the values of local control and "participatory democracy" are not embodied in a coherent program and strategy for change, a theoretical understanding of postindustrial society, and an alternative culture and vision. As long as the Left merely reacts to events, exposing and disrupting the "system" without offering anything to take its place, it suffers endless defeats and frustrations out of which grows, not a consciousness of alternatives, but a rising demand for more and more militant tactics. The worst features of the Old Left then begin to reappear in the New: dogmatism, an obsession with factional purity, vilification of opponents, hysterical gestures of alienation, the cult of violence. Eventually the New Left loses sight of its own peculiar traditions of local autonomy and democratic decision-making; New Left organizations begin to resemble the autocratic bureaucracies of the Stalinist period, against which SDS and other groups originally rebelled.

The experience of the New Left already refutes one of its principal tenets, that a revolutionary movement has no need of theory because theory will spring spontaneously out of the daily struggles of the movement. Struggle itself leads only to more struggle, or—as in the case of the labor unions—to eventual absorption. Particularly in a society for which no kind of precedent exists, the problems of which, accordingly, are almost entirely novel, a theory of social change can develop only if radicals—particularly radical intellectuals—cultivate it systematically. The United States is a society in which capitalism itself, by solving the problem of capital accumulation, has created the material conditions for a humane and democratic socialism, but in which the consciousness of alternatives to capitalism, once so pervasive, has almost faded from memory. This contradiction will not disappear in the course of struggle against capitalism, unless the struggle is carried into the realm of ideology and becomes a demand not merely for equality and justice but for a new culture, absorbing but transcending the old.

INDEX

Aaron, Daniel: on *Masses,* 48; on art and politics, 50
academic freedom, 95–6; Hook on, 82–4; ACCF on, 83; in RAND, 114
Addams, Jane, 10
Affluent Society, The (Galbraith), 195
alienation: of intellectuals, 46; and New Left, 144 *n.;* in 1950's, 180 *n.;* of students, 186–7
Alliance for Progress, 81
American Committee for Cultural Freedom (ACCF), 78–94; founding, 78; internal conflict in, 80–1; on academic freedom, 83; criticizes McCarthy, 86; on "anti-anticommunism," 87; on Rosenberg case, 87; guidelines for dissent, 87–8; on US and USSR, 90; on censorship, 91; criticizes US officials, 91–3; on academic freedom, 93–4; *see also* Congress for Cultural Freedom
American Federation of Labor, 17–18, 23
American Friends of the Middle East, 100
American Legion, 91
American Newspaper Guild, 100
Anderson, Sherwood, 54
Anthony, Susan B.: quoted, 25
"anti-anticommunism," 87, 88 *n.*
anticommunism, 82; as attack on

bourgeoisie, 68; as pragmatism, 69; as populism, 85–6
Appeal to Reason, The, 35
Aptheker, Herbert, 55, 72 *n.*
Army-McCarthy hearings, 86
Arneson, Richard J.: quoted, 181–2
Arnold, G. L., 64 *n.*
Atlantis (Donnelly), 15
Atomic Energy Commission, 92
Auden, W. H., 76
Axel's Castle (Wilson), 53
Ayer, A. J., 64

Baker, Newton D., 10
Bay of Pigs, 73 and *n.,* 81–2, 205
Bazelon, David T., 196–7
Beard, Charles A., 7
Bell, Daniel, 80, 171–2
Benda, Julian, 73
Berger, Victor, 38–9
Berkeley Barb, 202
Berkeley student revolt, 176, 184–6
Berle, Adolph A., 44
Biderman, Albert D., 113–14
Black Jews, 127
Black Muslims: *see* Nation of Islam
black nationalism, 126–8; and socialism, 41; and black power, 128–31; and ghetto, 144–5; escapist tendencies, 164–6; and young men, 165–6
Black Panther Party, 207
black power, 117–68 *passim;* and civil rights movement, 117–28;

A NOTE ABOUT THE AUTHOR

CHRISTOPHER LASCH was born in Omaha, Nebraska, in 1932. He attended Harvard (B.A. 1954) and Columbia University (M.A. 1955, Ph.D. 1961) and has taught history at Williams College 1957–9), Roosevelt University (1960–1), and at the State University of Iowa, where he was appointed associate professor in 1963. In 1966 he became Professor of History at Northwestern University. Winner of the Bowdoin Prize of Harvard in 1954, he has held both the Erb Fellowship (1955–6) and the Gilder Fellowship (1956–7) at Columbia University. Mr. Lasch is the author of two previous books, *The American Liberals and the Russian Revolution* (1962) and *The New Radicalism in America* (1965). He has contributed many articles to *The New York Review of Books* and other periodicals and journals. He now lives in Evanston, Illinois, with his wife, the former Nell Commager, and their four children.

A NOTE ON THE TYPE

THIS BOOK was set on the Linotype in *Granjon,* a type named in compliment to Robert Granjon, but neither a copy of a classic face nor an entirely original creation. GEORGE W. JONES based his designs for this type upon the type used by Claude Garamond (1510–61) in his beautiful French books, and Granjon more closely resembles Garamond's own than do any of the various modern types that bear his name.

Robert Granjon began his career as type-cutter in 1523. The boldest and most original designer of his time, he was one of the first to practice the trade of type-founder apart from that of printer. Between 1557 and 1562 Granjon printed about twenty books in types designed by himself, following, after the fashion of the day, the cursive handwriting of the time. These types, usually known as "caractères de civilité," he himself called "lettres françaises," as especially appropriate to his own country.

The book was composed, printed, and bound by
The Haddon Craftsmen, Scranton, Pennsylvania
Typography and binding design by
GUY FLEMING